W9-BTG-129

PR 3724 G8 B7

Brady, Frank, WITHDRAWN 84-285

Twentieth century
  interpretations of

		JUL	2000
		JUN	2004
		JUN 09	
		JUL X X 2015	

TWENTIETH CENTURY
INTERPRETATIONS
MAYNARD MACK, *Series Editor*
Yale University

NOW AVAILABLE
Collections of Critical Essays
ON

ADVENTURES OF HUCKLEBERRY FINN
ALL FOR LOVE
ARROWSMITH
AS YOU LIKE IT
THE BOOK OF JOB
THE DUCHESS OF MALFI
THE FROGS
SIR GAWAIN AND THE GREEN KNIGHT
THE GREAT GATSBY
GULLIVER'S TRAVELS
HAMLET
HENRY IV, PART TWO
HENRY V
THE ICEMAN COMETH
THE PORTRAIT OF A LADY
SAMSON AGONISTES
THE SCARLET LETTER
THE SOUND AND THE FURY
TOM JONES
TWELFTH NIGHT
UTOPIA
WALDEN
THE WASTE LAND

TWENTIETH CENTURY INTERPRETATIONS
OF

GULLIVER'S TRAVELS

TWENTIETH CENTURY INTERPRETATIONS
OF

GULLIVER'S TRAVELS

A Collection of Critical Essays

Edited by

FRANK BRADY

CUMBERLAND COUNTY COLLEGE
LIBRARY P.O. BOX 517 VINELAND N.J.

Prentice-Hall, Inc. *Englewood Cliffs, N. J.*

A SPECTRUM BOOK

PR
3724
G8
B7

84-265

Copyright © 1968 by Prentice-Hall, Inc., Englewood Cliffs, New Jersey. A SPEC-
TRUM BOOK. All rights reserved. No part of this book may be reproduced in any
form or by any means without permission in writing from the publisher. *Library
of Congress Catalog Card Number 68-23699.* Printed in the United States of
America.

Current printing (last number):
10 9 8 7 6 5 4 3 2 1

Contents

TWENTIETH CENTURY INTERPRETATIONS
OF

GULLIVER'S TRAVELS

Full Names of Journals
Abbreviated in Footnotes

HLQ	*Huntington Library Quarterly*
MLN	*Modern Language Notes*
MP	*Modern Philology*
PQ	*Philological Quarterly*
SP	*Studies in Philology*
UTQ	*University of Toronto Quarterly*

Introduction

by Frank Brady

I

The one story everyone knows about *Gulliver's Travels* is that an Irish bishop said it "was full of improbable lies, and for his part he hardly believed a word of it." [1] In the literal-minded eighteenth century, when fact was often equated with truth and fiction with lie, this remark must have seemed even more peculiar than it does now. But the story still gives readers from freshmen to experienced critics a reassuring sense of superiority not always justified by their own interpretations of the work. By accident at least, the bishop had a point. Granted that big men and little men don't literally exist, the question remains, "What are we to believe about *Gulliver's Travels?*"

The answer to this question, as to most major questions about the work, lies in what one decides about the relationship between Swift and Gulliver. Are their views identical by the end of the Fourth Voyage, as most nineteenth-century critics assumed? Or are their views completely divergent by then, as many modern critics think? To what extent does Swift sustain the idea that Lemuel Gulliver is writing his own travels? Does Gulliver have a consistent character, or even what can be called a "character" at all? Is it possible to discover Swift's opinions, or is *Gulliver's Travels* a prosaic analogue of *Hamlet,* a mirror in which each reader sees his own reflection?

This introduction does not contain solutions to these problems; it can only indicate two approaches to them. One starts with Swift's life and works, and broadens to consider the intellectual and literary history of the period. The other concentrates on *Gulliver* as a work in itself. Loosely, these can be called external and internal approaches.

The external approach first. *Gulliver's Travels* was published anonymously in London by Benjamin Motte late in 1726. Its popularity was immediate and its authorship soon widely known. Swift, at this time almost sixty, was the Anglican Dean of St. Patrick's Cathedral, Dublin. Of English parentage, he had been born and educated in

---

[1] Swift to Pope [27 Nov. 1726].

1

Ireland, graduating from Trinity College. For several years he had been confidential secretary to the essayist and retired diplomat, Sir William Temple; during this period he took orders and briefly held various Irish livings. Later he represented the Irish bishops in London, joining the Tories there and becoming good friends with their leaders, Oxford and Bolingbroke. His hope to be made a bishop was frustrated, according to an old story, by Queen Anne's dislike of the supposedly irreligious aspects of his early, brilliant work, *A Tale of a Tub*. (From the beginning, Swift's readers have had difficulty in distinguishing the straightforward from the ironic.) He was, however, made Dean of St. Patrick's, and after the Tories fell in 1714 he returned to spend almost all the rest of his life in—as he headed one letter—"wretched Dublin in miserable Ireland."

Here, in disappointment and isolation, Swift devoted much of his time to supporting the Irish against their English masters. As "M. B., Drapier," he led the fight against the imposition of Wood's halfpence, which he asserted would ruin the Irish monetary system; his success made him a national hero. Again and again he unavailingly urged economic reform for Ireland, and the extent of his eventual loss of hope is suggested in *A Modest Proposal*. His mixed attitude of protectiveness and contempt toward the Irish is caught in the closing lines of his "Verses on the Death of Dr. Swift":

> "He gave the little wealth he had,
> To build a house for fools and mad;
> And showed by one satiric touch,
> No nation wanted it so much."

An equally mixed attitude toward mankind may appear in *Gulliver's Travels*.

Apart from the obscurities of his long relationship with Esther Johnson (Stella), the facts of Swift's life are fairly clear. His complex temperament and personality, however, tend to elude and sometimes repel readers. In religion and politics, he was a conservative, a believer in the authority of church and state. He thought the general and traditional wisdom embodied in these institutions corrected the inherent biases of the individual mind. But he realized that institutions might themselves be corrupted, and he had no illusions about the specific kings, ministers, and bishops who directed them. He believed in common sense rather than in systems or in abstract reasoning: he disliked anything theoretical in approach, including metaphysics and what we now call science, as irrelevant to man's central moral concerns. At the same time, common sense led him to distrust "enthusiasm," the contemporary term for any kind of fanatical or even highly emotional attitude or behavior.

On such general points there is little dispute about Swift's attitudes. No similar agreement exists about the attitudes toward mankind expressed in *Gulliver's Travels*. The *locus classicus* of discussion occurs in a letter to Pope (29 September 1725):

> The chief end I propose to myself in all my labors is to vex the world rather than divert it. . . . I have ever hated all nations, professions, and communities, and all my love is toward individuals: for instance, I hate the tribe of lawyers, but I love Counsellor Such-a-one, Judge Such-a-one: for so with physicians (I will not speak of my own trade), soldiers, English, Scotch, French, and the rest. But principally I hate and detest that animal called man, although I heartily love John, Peter, Thomas, and so forth. This is the system upon which I have governed myself many years (but do not tell) and so I shall go on till I have done with them. I have got materials towards a treatise, proving the falsity of that definition *animal rationale*, and to show it should be only *rationis capax*. Upon this great foundation of misanthropy (though not Timon's manner), the whole building of my *Travels* is erected; and I never will have peace of mind till all honest men are of my opinion. By consequence you are to embrace it immediately, and procure that all who deserve my esteem may do so too. The matter is so clear that it will admit little dispute; nay, I will hold a hundred pounds that you and I agree on the point.

As a gloss on *Gulliver*, this much quoted passage darkens under our eyes. First, its meaning seems clearer than it is. What does Swift have in mind when he says he hates collective entities and loves individuals? He may imply 1) any group acts according to its lowest common denominator; 2) individuality disappears when one adopts the pose or attitude or mask of the group; 3) "that animal called man" is naturally detestable, though individuals can be lovable. Or he may just imply that he hates generalizations about people. Also, the distinction between *animal rationale* (rational animal) and *rationis capax* ([animal] capable of reasoning) may be clear in theory, but it offers neither an easy nor a comprehensive guide to *Gulliver's Travels*. Who there illustrates that man is *rationis capax?* Gulliver? The King of Brobdingnag? Pedro de Mendez? or the reader?

Second, Swift's irony, characteristically cutting a number of ways, includes himself. He calls his view of man a "great foundation of misanthropy," though of course he and his contemporaries considered misanthropy one of the worst vices. His insistence that Pope adopt his opinion "immediately" seems both a serious attitude and a self-directed parody of Gulliver's belief that "seven months were a sufficient time to correct every vice and folly" (Gulliver, to his Cousin Sympson). Where irony holds two attitudes in suspension, no decisive interpretation of a passage is possible.

Finally, even if it were possible to reach agreement on the passage's meaning, no single passage could explain so complicated a work as *Gulliver*. At best it could offer hints toward interpretation that would have to be weighed against other evidence. A relevant example is Swift's subsequent comment in a letter to Pope (26 November 1725):

> I tell you after all that I do not hate mankind; it is *vous autres* who hate them, because you would have them reasonable animals and are angry for being disappointed.

The parallels cited to *Gulliver* from Swift's other works are about as helpful as Swift quoted on himself. For example, in considering Swift's relationship to Gulliver, it is common to urge as analogous the use of a spokesman or *persona* whose views differ from Swift's own, like the tale-teller in *A Tale of a Tub* or the businessman in *A Modest Proposal*. The trouble is that no consistent divergence can be established between Swift's views and those of his *personae;* the distance between them varies according to the rhetorical requirements of each work. Such analogies tell the reader where to look for the point rather than what the point is.

To move from Swift to the political history of his time brings greater certainty. Commentators generally agree, for instance, that Flimnap represents the Prime Minister, Sir Robert Walpole, and that Laputa and Balnibarbi portray England and Ireland. (Lindalino, the capital of Balnibarbi, is double "lin.") Where doubt exists, as about the historical counterpart of Reldresal, the loss to the general reader is slight.

In contrast to the relative unimportance of these specific political references, the intellectual attitudes presented in *Gulliver's Travels* and their philosophic bases have become the most significant area for modern discussion of the work. This discussion began in 1926 when T. O. Wedel argued that Swift held a traditional Christian view of man and not some peculiarly misanthropic one, and that in the Houyhnhnms he satirized the increasingly popular optimistic concept of human nature exemplified in deism. In 1941, J. F. Ross extended this argument in "The Final Comedy of Lemuel Gulliver" by carefully dissociating Swift from Gulliver's ultimate misanthropy, and this line of reasoning has become widely accepted. Recent rejoinders to it are illustrated here by R. S. Crane's "The Houyhnhnms, the Yahoos, and the History of Ideas." [2]

An evident gain from this disagreement has been an increase in sophistication. Scholars, once content to interpret the work through

---

[2] For two more complex views, see Martin Price, *Swift's Rhetorical Art* (New Haven: Yale University Press, 1953), especially pp. 100–102; and John Traugott, "A Voyage to Nowhere with Thomas More and Jonathan Swift: *Utopia* and *The Voyage to the Houyhnhnms*," *Sewanee Review*, 69 (1961), 534–65.

their own intuitions, have been forced to examine it in terms of the period's theological and philosophical concerns. A similar growth in awareness appears in studies of the literary background of *Gulliver*. The rather simpleminded investigation of sources and analogues popular in the early part of this century has been replaced by the realization that, generically speaking, *Gulliver* is a complex amalgam of several literary forms: real and imaginary voyages, allegory including the beast fable, and satire. As a result, critics today are less liable to make inappropriate demands on the work. It is illogical, for example, to expect satiric allegory to present character and incident in the same fashion as the realistic novel. But at this point we start to shift from the study of what lies behind or around the work to the study of the work itself.

II

It would be pleasant to believe, as Coleridge did, that "the feelings of the reader will be his faithful guide in the reperusal" of *Gulliver's Travels*.[3] Experience suggests, however, that anyone who relies on such feelings had better be as sophisticated as Swift himself. It is more useful to try to approach the work as if it were new, to see it as one of Swift's original readers might have. Perhaps he was struck first by "the extraordinary illusion of verisimilitude"[4] in which Swift launches Gulliver and strands him on Lilliput, and the sideslip into fantasy as Gulliver finds the "declivity" of the beach so gentle that he walks "near a mile" to shore, and lies down on the "very short and soft" grass. Yet the shock of fantasy is mitigated by Gulliver's immediate recognition of "a human creature not six inches high" (I.i).

This reader would delight, as contemporary reactions show, in the playfulness and ingenuity of Swift's imagination. (Dr. Johnson was to remark with serene injustice, "When once you have thought of big men and little men, it is very easy to do all the rest."[5]) Much of the enjoyment comes from precision of phrasing, as in Reldresal's title, "Principal Secretary of Private Affairs," which neatly reflects the busy, gossipy world of Augustan politics. Other phrases cut more deeply. After Gulliver describes in detail how he first "disburthened" himself in Lilliput, he continues, "When this adventure was at an end . . ." (I.ii). Here Swift has mocked not only the heroic doings of travelers in far-off lands but also the general human sense of self-importance in

[3] T. M. Raysor, ed., *Coleridge's Miscellaneous Criticism* (London: Constable & Co., Ltd., 1936), p. 130.

[4] R. C. Elliott's phrase in *The Power of Satire* (Princeton: Princeton University Press, 1960), p. 197.

[5] James Boswell, *Life of Samuel Johnson*, 24 Mar. 1775.

its own "productions." These are the "particulars" which "will certainly help a philosopher to enlarge his thoughts and imagination" (II.i).

In general, the reader would be likely to identify with Gulliver in his travels, even while recognizing his naiveté in the First Voyage and vanity in the Second. Depending on the extent of this identification, he might be angered or upset by the conclusion of the Fourth Voyage, a victim of what H. W. Sams calls "satire of the second person." Finally, and most important to our purposes, he might well be puzzled. The movement from fantasy to "reality" and back again generates the meaning of *Gulliver's Travels* and also some of its problems: the complex relationships of literal and figurative, the presentation of Gulliver's character, the dazzling and often ambiguous potentialities of irony and literalization.

Fantasy is the literal level of *Gulliver's Travels* and, as the Irish bishop discovered, this level offers problems in itself. Gulliver arrives in Lilliput in a shower of circumstantial detail, most of it apparently accurate on its 1 : 12 scale. Yet the closer one looks at it, the less convincing the detail seems. For example, Gulliver's handkerchief, two and one-half feet square, supposedly supports 24 Lilliputian horsemen (I.iii), though the horses alone are four and one-half inches high (I.i). This is barely possible, but if horses and oxen are between four inches and five inches high, then sheep can hardly be only one and one-half inches high (I.vi.). What is even more improbable, Gulliver tows 50 Blefuscudian warships "with great ease" to Lilliput (I.v), though the largest are nine feet long (I.i). (In contrast, Gulliver has a severe struggle to beach the "real" boat on which he leaves Blefuscu.)

Perhaps these are merely slips in detail, though it seems unlikely that anyone who could imagine a four and one-half inch horse would forget to envisage a proportionately sized sheep. Similarly, as J. R. Moore demonstrates, the general geographical details of Gulliver's voyages are fantastic. One explanation of these anomalies is that Swift is parodying the wild detail found in contemporary travelers' accounts, but an alternative or further explanation is suggested by one incident. Gulliver defends himself against the Treasurer by asserting that he never received anyone incognito except Reldresal (I.vi). Three paragraphs later, Gulliver describes in detail the incognito visit of "a considerable person at court" (I.vii). Authors are seldom this forgetful; presumably the reader is supposed to pick up the contradiction, which implies that Gulliver is a liar. Most readers, of course, pass over this incident without noticing it, but then the work as a whole constantly tests the reader's gullibility as well as illustrating the hero's.

To show that Gulliver is a liar early in the work may indicate no more than that he will go to considerable length to defend his reputation, as well as that of the Treasurer's wife. In the Second Voyage, he admits that he shades the facts about England in his "laudable partiality" to his native country (II.vii). The Gulliver who is "distinguished for his veracity" (the Publisher to the Reader) does not emerge until he has acquired the Houyhnhnm love of truth or, more accurately, ignorance of lying. Yet, when at the end of the Fourth Voyage Gulliver compares his truthfulness to Sinon's, the comparison is at best unfortunate since Sinon was the most celebrated liar of antiquity. And whoever adorned the frontispiece portrait of Gulliver in Faulkner's 1735 edition of Swift's *Works* with the legend, "*splendide mendax*" (gloriously false), must have had some suspicions.

Gulliver thinks of truthfulness in terms of literal fact. But in what G. Wilson Knight calls the "symbolic, sensory-physical structure" of *Gulliver's Travels,* the literal almost invariably carries a more significant metaphorical meaning. Damage to Gulliver's clothes, Paul Fussell points out, suggests his frailty. W. B. Carnochan similarly traces the relationship of Gulliver's "lack of understanding" to the "weakness and vulnerability of his eyesight." So when Gulliver remarks that the virtues of "those excellent quadrupeds," the Houyhnhnms, had "so far opened my eyes and enlarged my understanding that I began to view the actions and passions of man in a very different light" (IV.vii), the sight-perspective pattern already established gives the comment unexpected reverberations.[6]

Swift makes this basic point by simple inversion: Gulliver's retention of his "pocket perspective," or spyglass, in Lilliput symbolizes his loss of metaphorical perspective. In each voyage, he tends to lose his sense of identity as he assimilates himself to his new world and its creatures: as a Nardac in Lilliput he ranks himself higher than the Treasurer, "for all the world knows he is only a Clumglum" (I.vi); on his return from Brobdingnag he has lost all sense of human size; and in his final exile in England he more or less thinks he is a Houyhnhnm, or at least a horse. Even on the Third Voyage where he is at odds with his Laputian hosts, he takes on enough of their mental outlook to venture "astronomical" and etymological speculations. Introduced at the Grand Academy as "a person of much curiosity and easy belief," he investigates it with the interest of one who had been "a sort of projector in [his] younger days" (I.iv). Finally, his momentary metamorphosis into a Struldbrugg demonstrates the futility of trying to be other than a human being.

Significantly, Gulliver's hosts repeatedly reject the analogies between him and them that he is eager to make. In effect, they refuse to believe he is a fellow creature. It is true that the intellectuals of

[6] H. D. Kelling points to the significance of this comment in *"Gulliver's Travels: A Comedy of Humours," University of Toronto Quarterly,* 21 (1952), 371.

Laputa merely dismiss him as beneath notice, but the Lilliputians think him a "man-mountain" who has dropped from the moon or stars. The Brobdingnagians speculate that he is a clockwork toy or carnivorous animal or embryo, and conclude that he is *lusus naturae,* a freak of nature. The Houyhnhnms, of course, classify him as a Yahoo, an animal. Here for the first time, Gulliver consciously agrees with his hosts about himself.

Such traits as Gulliver's literal-mindedness and tendency toward assimilation imply that in some ways his character and attitudes remain consistent throughout the work, but the consistency of his character as a whole is much debated. Especially in the Third Voyage, Gulliver seems to assume rapidly varying points of view. He despises the agricultural experiments of Balnibarbi, but praises foolish projects in the Academy; in Glubbdubdrib, he alternates between demanding superficial "scenes of pomp and magnificence," and admiring the great "destroyers of tyrants and usurpers" (III.vii).

One difference between the novel and satire is that satire demands consistency in underlying viewpoint rather than in character; our interest is rather in what is said than in who says it. At the same time, as Northrop Frye has suggested, a certain kind of satire presupposes a certain kind of protagonist: "a plain common-sense conventional person as a foil for the various *alazons* [impostors] of society." [7] This description fits the sturdy, practical, rather insensitive Gulliver who is sketched at the beginning of the work, so it is all the more bewildering when Gulliver himself starts to play the *alazon*.[8] This difficulty has led R. C. Elliott to argue that Gulliver is "an abstraction manipulated in the service of satire," and Kathleen Williams to say that, in Laputa, "he ceases to have any character and, in effect, vanishes." Perhaps more accurately, his character vanishes and reappears erratically, like the grin of the Cheshire Cat.[9]

What we do know of Gulliver's character is largely determined by the disparity between him and the peoples he visits, which Swift exploits as a ready-made ironic device. Here again, literal often plays against figurative. To cite two examples connected with the loss of perspective pattern discussed earlier: when Gulliver reports that the

---

[7] *Anatomy of Criticism* (Princeton: Princeton University Press, 1957), p. 226. A. B. Kernan describes the typical satiric protagonist in interesting detail in *The Cankered Muse* (New Haven: Yale University Press, 1959), pp. 14–30.

[8] This now commonplace view of Gulliver is argued in extreme form by J. R. Wilson, "Swift's Alazon," *Studia neophilologica,* 30 (1958), 153–64.

[9] Ian Watt suggests there are "inherent contradictions between the functions of the ironic *persona* and the fully developed literary character" ("The Ironic Tradition in Augustan Prose" in J. R. Sutherland and Ian Watt, *Restoration & Augustan Prose,* [Los Angeles: William Andrews Clark Memorial Library, 1956], p. 32).

Lilliputians "see with great exactness, but at no great distance" (I.vi), physical shortsightedness parallels moral pettiness and insensitivity. In a more complicated instance, Gulliver's waving of his scimitar dazzles the eyes of the Lilliputians, but at the same time he fails to observe 3,000 troops drawn up to guard him because his eyes "were wholly fixed" upon the Emperor (I.ii).

Irony here is easily recognizable because the context of the First Voyage firmly establishes the standards to be shared by author and reader. Where standards are less explicit, the reader is sometimes in difficulty. In the Second Voyage, Gulliver laughs at "a little old treatise . . . of morality and devotion" (II.vii), which draws moral lessons from the physical degeneration of nature, but critics have been uncertain whether to laugh with him. What should we think when Gulliver says, "I could not avoid reflecting how universally this talent was spread of drawing lectures in morality, or indeed rather matter of discontent and repining, from the quarrels we raise with nature"?

This opinion actually involves two contexts, that of the Voyage to Brobdingnag (in which Gulliver is generally the object of satire), and that of Swift's general views on the degeneration of nature. (Here internal and external approaches to the work overlap.) Swift may have held some cyclic version of history, in which society goes through stages of growth and decline like individuals. Or he may have taken the common view that nature, including society and its institutions, was in a process of decay. One critic claims that "deteriorationism" is one of the most important motifs of *Gulliver's Travels*.[10]

Yet the evidence is conflicting. When Gulliver on Glubbdubdrib compares past and present, he remarks typically: "It gave me melancholy reflections to observe how much the race of human kind was degenerate among us, within these hundred years past" (III.viii). Just previously, he gave at length the story of Augustus's ingratitude toward one of his ship commanders, a cautionary tale that implies history is cyclic. Degenerative and cyclic views of history can be made to jibe, but when Gulliver, indulging in Struldbruggian visions, thinks he could help "prevent that continual degeneracy of human nature so justly complained of in all ages" (III.x), context and the overdone rhetoric of "continual" and "justly" suggest that Swift does not believe in the degeneration of nature. Or, more likely, he wants it both ways: Gulliver's potted simplifications of history are absurd, but the Moderns, if not in a state of continuous degeneration, are still inferior to the Ancients.[11]

---

[10] Z. S. Fink, "Political Theory in *Gulliver's Travels*," *ELH*, 14 (1947), 161. For a different view, see Ernest Tuveson, "Swift: The Dean as Satirist," *University of Toronto Quarterly*, 22 (1953), 374.

[11] See Kelling, *op. cit.*, p. 370.

Certainly Swift's ability to make irony work in a number of direc-
tions at once is a major cause of confusion about the Fourth Voyage.
Readers of satire are conditioned to think in right-wrong, either-or
terms; Swift demands that we think in both-and terms. According to
many modern critics, the problem is not whether Gulliver is right in
idealizing the Houyhnhnms, but whether he is both right and wrong,
and to what extent.

The central ironic device of the Fourth Voyage is literalization, the
reduction of the symbolic or mental to the physical, or the treatment of
the metaphorical as if it were literal. A simple instance is Gulliver's
reduction of the crucifix to "a post" (IV.v). The reverse procedure is
also possible: the literal becomes metaphoric. Gulliver expects to find
savages and instead finds the Yahoos, who are "savage by nature"
(IV.ix). He takes the first Houyhnhnms he meets for metamorphosed
magicians, and there are reasons for arguing that the Houyhnhnms
turn him into a Yahoo, as Circe turned men into swine. When he
arrives at the Houyhnhnm house, he rubs his eyes and pinches himself
because he thinks he is dreaming; later Pedro de Mendez suggests that
the whole voyage is "a dream or a vision" (IV.xi).

Literalization occurs most significantly, of course, when that "rational animal," man, confronts a literally rational animal for whom
"nature and reason [are] sufficient guides" (IV.v). And, at the same
time, man is allowed to equate himself with a totally irrational animal.
By manipulating these three elements, man, Houyhnhnm, and Yahoo,
Swift develops complicated ironic effects, of which simpler examples,
discussed earlier, arise from the disparity between Gulliver and the
Lilliputians. When Gulliver's Houyhnhnm master illuminates human
avarice by equating it with the Yahoos' habit of piling up "shining
stones" (IV.vii), he satirizes both humans and Yahoos.[12] But this account also satirizes Gulliver and the Houyhnhnm, since they fail to
recognize that it reduces money from a unit of exchange to a physical
object.

Literal-figurative correspondences in extended narrative produce
allegory. But where allegory usually depends on a simple likeness or
discrepancy between literal and figurative levels, the Houyhnhnms
offer a special case: they are simultaneously horses, "rational animals,"
and to some extent the representatives of human ideals. So the impression they convey, instead of being fixed, varies in accordance with
the way these three elements are juxtaposed. When their physical and
mental attributes are congruent, as in the account of their education
and physical training, they appear admirable; their four cardinal vir-

---

[12] Strictly speaking, the Yahoos are satirized only to the extent they are assimilated
to human beings. As Bergson pointed out, animal behavior in itself is never comic.

tues, "temperance, industry, exercise, and cleanliness" (IV.viii), are appropriate ones. When horsiness and rationality seem in conflict, the effect may be to satirize both them and human beings: the first Houyhnhnms to meet Gulliver, he says, "were under great perplexity about my shoes and stockings, which they felt very often, neighing to each other, and using various gestures, not unlike those of a philosopher, when he would attempt to solve some new and difficult phenomenon" (IV.i). And when the Houyhnhnms perform specifically human actions, such as sitting on their haunches and threading needles, they seem comic. In contrast, when the pigs in *Animal Farm* imitate humans by sleeping in beds and walking on two feet, they seem both proud and sinister. The Houyhnhnms' pride appears, instead, in their assumption of total superiority. (Coleridge, trusting his feelings, indignantly pointed out the superiority of the hand to the hoof.)

While the significance as well as the nature of the Houyhnhnms may be double, triple, or just problematic, there is little unequivocal about Gulliver's reaction to Houyhnhnmland. He believes that physically he is a Yahoo, but rejects this identification metaphorically by making bird traps, shoes, a canoe, and sails, of their skins and "tallow." On the other hand, the Houyhnhnms become "amiable persons" deserving the "highest veneration" (IV.x). This Gulliver shows when he starts to prostrate himself before his Master upon departing; he is worshiping a beast god.

The human world Gulliver returns to comments on his earlier experiences. He is first attacked by savages, whom he had anticipated meeting in Houyhnhnmland, and then rescued by the Portuguese sailors, who speak to him "with great humanity." Their captain, Pedro de Mendez, gives Gulliver the well-aired shirt off his back and, in response, Gulliver says, "I descended to treat him like an animal which had some little portion of reason" (IV.xi).

So this grim charade ends with Gulliver, a literalist of the imagination, set in his horselike ways and very reluctant to rejoin humanity. It seems likely that we are meant to apply to him—we are certainly meant to apply it to somebody—what he says of Captain Pocock: "He was an honest man, and a good sailor, but a little too positive in his own opinions, which was the cause of his destruction, as it hath been of several others" (IV.i). Whether Swift loved or hated humanity, he was able, unlike Gulliver, to look it straight in the face.

PART ONE

Interpretations

The Sources of *Gulliver's Travels*

by Milton Voigt

If studies of the sources of *Gulliver's Travels* have not always brought a more complete understanding of Swift's work, it must be allowed that the more rewarding of these studies made no such promise. Rather, they were intended as modest contributions to the larger task of understanding which "lay ahead." This important phase of literary scholarship, now suffering a not wholly deserved disrepute, grew from a conviction popular in nineteenth-century Germany that literary— no less than social and natural—phenomena, being moments in a larger process of change and growth, could be understood only as a phase of evolutionary development from stimulus to response, early groping to later discovery, inchoate matter to final synthesis. Thus *Gulliver's Travels* was to be understood as a development from a complex of origins. These origins were primarily literary, though other influences were to be traced, particularly those revealed in biographical and historical research. When early students of Swift's sources, aware apparently of the immensity of their task, proceeded with what was manifestly an inadequate or even nonexistent understanding of the work whose literary relationships they sought to establish, a certain modesty was only proper. The meaning and character of the work were to be examined by a method which was by definition piece-meal. As time went on, amidst many false starts and wide disagreements, certain literary and philosophical relationships were established. These relationships contributed to our knowledge of literary and cultural history and of Swift's place in it.

There had been interest in the sources and predecessors of *Gulliver's Travels* long before the pursuit of indebtedness became scientifically earnest. Orrery, Scott, Monck Mason, and others had commented on the question of *Gulliver's* sources before 1868, when Canon E. H.

"The Sources of Gulliver's Travels*" by Milton Voigt. From* Swift and the Twentieth Century *(Detroit: Wayne State University Press, 1964), pp. 65–76. Copyright © 1964 by the Wayne State University Press. Reprinted by permission of the author and publisher.*

Knowles made what must have seemed an auspicious discovery. In *Notes and Queries* for that year,[1] he asked whether anyone had previously called attention to Swift's use of a passage in Sturmy's *Compleat Mariner* (1669), a passage which appeared in *Gulliver* almost verbatim as the description of the storm early in the voyage to Brobdingnag. Few subsequent researchers have been able to point to parallel passages with similar certainty. Knowles's discovery was perhaps an unfortunate example for later students, who were led to search for just such merely verbal parallels or parallels of incident or narrative. Source hunting of this type, so often futile and inconclusive when applied to Swift, led to a yet more mistaken type of study, of which Borkowsky's "Quellen zu Swifts *Gulliver*" (1893)[2] is a good example.

Borkowsky, ostensibly working in the best tradition of *Quellen Studien*, was actually more interested in destroying what he considered to be Swift's undeserved reputation for originality than in establishing Swift's literary relationships. Offering Sturmy and other parallel passages as evidence, Borkowsky apparently hoped to demonstrate that Swift was as dependent upon his sources as Coleridge was upon German philosophers. Indebtedness to More's *Utopia*, Rabelais, Denis Vairasse d'Alais' *L'Histoire des Sévarambes* (1677–79), Gabriel de Foigny's *La Terre australe connue* (1676), and especially Cyrano de Bergerac's *L'Histoire comique de la lune* (1656) was asserted, and relevant passages were compared. For the indebtedness to Cyrano— which had been noted as early as Orrery[3] and more extensively analyzed by Henry Wilson[4]—Borkowsky relied largely upon the more judicious study by Hönncher,[5] which had appeared in *Anglia* in 1888. Though Borkowsky's purpose was primarily to analyze Swift's sources, he also asserted Swift's authorship of *A Voyage to Cacklogallinia* (1727), a desperate conjecture not strengthened by its being based wholly upon a German translation of the work.

Several discussions of sources appeared in the decade following G. Ravenscroft Dennis' edition (1899) of *Gulliver*, the introduction to which included a succinct summary of *Gulliver*'s sources as understood at the turn of the century. In the same year a more detailed review was offered by Paul Thierkopf, *Swifts Gulliver und seine französischen Vorgänger*. An American study, Max Poll's *The Sources of "Gulliver's Travels,"* appeared in 1904, followed in 1906–7 by yet another collation and summary of source criticism, Pietro Toldo's

[1] 4th series, 1 (1868), 223.
[2] *Anglia*, 15 (1893), 345–89.
[3] *Remarks*, 1752, p. 145.
[4] Wilson's revision of J. C. Dunlop, *The History of Fiction*, 1888, ii, 525–36.
[5] Erwin Hönncher, "Quellen zu Dean Swifts *Gulliver's Travels*," *Anglia*, 10 (1888), 297–427.

"Les Voyages merveilleux de Cyrano de Bergerac et de Swift et leurs rapports avec l'oeuvre de Rabelais." Toldo, besides dealing with Rabelais and Cyrano, took up Swift's relationship to Lucian, More, and Campanella, and pointed out numerous parallels with *The Arabian Nights,* particularly its story of Hassan-al-Bassri, which includes a visit to a land of giants.[6]

William Alfred Eddy's *Gulliver's Travels: A Critical Study,* generally regarded as definitive on the sources, appeared in 1923. Eddy, unlike his predecessors, pursued his research in the light of an explicit but mistaken interpretation of Swift's work, derived primarily from a misconception of Swift's intention. Eddy, seeing that *Gulliver* was in many ways similar to the imaginary voyage of philosophic intent, especially well-represented in French literature, classified it with that genre. He set about to establish systematically the literary relationships between *Gulliver* and other members of its class. However, the parallel passages and the similarities of incident and "conception" which he discovered in works such as Cyrano's *L'Histoire comique de la lune* and *L'Histoire comique du soleil* were merely superficial, for Swift was parodying incidents, conceptions, and especially the *Tendenz* of a tradition to which he was altogether hostile. The French philosophic voyages, of which Cyrano's are good examples, satirized civilization and Christianity in order to glorify natural man, natural "society," and natural, or deistic, religion. Eddy failed to perceive that if Swift used Cyrano and the tradition of the philosophic voyage, he did so to subvert the tradition, not to extend it.[7]

Eddy's misconception of *Gulliver* was not wholly disastrous to his purpose, but it sometimes leads him to dubious decisions on Swift's indebtedness to other works. Thus he contemptuously rejects Churton Collins' assertion that "several strokes for the Yahoos were borrowed from the *Travels* of Sir Thomas Herbert," [8] pointing out that Herbert's "is a dull book" and that Swift's low opinion of the work, recorded on the flyleaf of Swift's own copy, "does not indicate that Swift caught much inspiration from the reading" (p. 66, nn. 73–74). The "inspiration," if one wishes to call it that, which Swift "caught," is of the same order as that which Swift caught in another connection from Anthony Collins' *Discourse of Freethinking,* which, surely, is a "source" for Swift's parody of it, rendered into "Plain English . . . for Use of the Poor."

When discussing the possibility of a connection between *Gulliver* and Segrais' *L'Isle imaginaire* (1658), Eddy sets Segrais aside on

[6] *Revue des études rabelaisiennes,* 4 (1906), 295–304; 5 (1907), 24–44.

[7] A. M. Taylor, "Cyrano de Bergerac and Gulliver's Voyage to Brobdingnag," *Tulane Studies in English,* 5 (1955), 83–102, explores this thoroughly.

[8] J. C. Collins, *Jonathan Swift,* 1893, p. 205.

similarly questionable grounds. Eddy finds that Segrais' work, which
includes a republic of dogs,

> is not a sincere representation of cultivated animals; it is a burlesque,
> a deliberate parody of ideal commonwealths. Segrais felt the want of
> logic and truth in the exaggerated virtue and wisdom attributed to
> remote peoples by travellers. Why not as well, he implies, attribute
> utopian government to a race of dogs? Consequently we have repre-
> sented a Republic of Dogs, but one which is ostensibly a joke. It is not
> to be supposed that the traveller really discovered these dogs, and the
> reader is not asked to credit their remarkable virtues. I take it there is
> a genuine distinction here. The Houyhnhnms are of course fictitious,
> but the fiction is a serious one. Swift implies that their life is a model
> one, better than man's (pp. 182–83).

Having missed the ridicule of the philosophic imaginary voyage as a
genre, Eddy proceeds to miss the subtle ridicule of the utopias this
genre depicted.

The shortcomings of Eddy's work are more than offset by its exhaustiveness. Of the works credited as sources by his predecessors,
Eddy chooses to set aside Vairasse, Foigny, More, Godwin, and Herbert,
while retaining Lucian, Philostratus, Rabelais, and Cyrano. Eddy
justifies some of his rejections of earlier assertions of indebtedness on
the ground that the parallels of idea and incident are not peculiar to
the alleged source, but are common to the utopian voyage as a genre
(pp. 66–67, nn. 74, 77–78)—an argument which suggests that Swift, not
content with what he called "hints," was drawing, with truly prodigious
grasp, upon the tradition as a whole. Following up a conjecture by
E. N. S. Thompson,[9] Eddy suggests indebtedness to Tom Brown's
Amusements Serious and Comical (1700) for several experiments in
Lagado. He persuasively argues Swift's indebtedness to Lucian's *Voyage
to Heaven* for the device of inspecting objects from a great height, and
to the *Dialogues of the Dead* for the undesirability of immortality embodied in the Struldbrugg episode. Eddy finds in Cyrano's second ro-
mance, *L'Histoire comique du soleil,* which he analyzes more thoroughly than previous researchers had, adequate precedent for the
alleged scathing denunciation of mankind in the voyage to the Houyhnhnms. An important discovery is Swift's probable use of d'Ablancourt's French translation of Lucian, especially d'Ablancourt's con-
tinuation of the *True History,* which adds visits to "l'île des animaux
. . . quelle était environée de celle des géans, des magiciens, et des
pygmées." Most of the traceable similarities of narrative structure or
of incident present in other imaginary voyages, Eddy has laid bare.

---

[9] "Tom Brown and Eighteenth Century Satirists," *MLN,* 32 (1917), 90–94.

Eddy is lured away from the imaginary voyage and his preoccupation with purely literary sources when he fails to find a literary source for the "one fundamental idea" of the voyages to Lilliput and Brobdingnag. He defines this idea as "the relativity of human life and its values," and he traces it to Berkeley's *A New Theory of Vision* (1709). Here again, if a relationship exists at all, it is an extremely tenuous one. Lemuel Gulliver might conceivably draw upon relativist theory in order to point his moral or adorn his tale, as he does when exclaiming over the perspicuity of philosophers, who "undoubtedly . . . are in the right when they tell us that nothing is either great or little otherwise than by comparison" (II, i; HD, XI, 71),[10] but this is not to say, as Eddy does, that Swift in such instances is writing a tract in favor of relativism and that among the philosophers "undoubtedly in the right" is Swift's friend, George Berkeley.[11]

Two reviews of Eddy's work praised its exhaustiveness within the limits set but stressed the need for going beyond those limits. Émile Pons quarreled with Eddy's rough handling of some of his predecessors (especially Borkowsky) and with his dismissal of Swift's alleged indebtedness to More, Foigny, and Vairasse; but he was enthusiastic over Eddy's discovery of Swift's indebtedness to d'Ablancourt, though he found Eddy's analysis of this literary relationship less full than he had hoped for.[12] Pons regarded Eddy's distaste for the Houyhnhnms and the fourth voyage generally as a result of the inadequacy of Eddy's critical method and urged the use of biographical and psychological methods for the solution of the complex critical problem of the fourth voyage. A. W. Secord, also looking beyond relationships in the literary genre, regretted that Eddy, though willing to discuss Berkeley, Sturmy, and Herbert, none of whom wrote imaginary voyages, neglected native sources and traditions, especially authentic voyages.[13] Secord is inclined to accept Eddy's account, as far as it goes, of *Gulliver's* sources, though he objects to Eddy's rather equivocal handling of Holberg's *Journey of Klimius to the World Underground*.

Secord's suggestion that Gulliver owed much to authentic voyages was proved sound when studies by R. W. Frantz and Willard Bonner appeared in the thirties. Frantz, in "Swift's Yahoos and the Voyagers"

---

[10] References to *Gulliver* will indicate voyage and chapter, followed by citation to Herbert Davis' edn. of 1941.

[11] [For Swift and Berkeley, see H. C. Morris, *"The Dialogues of Hylas and Philonus* as a Source in *Gulliver's Travels,"* MLN, 70 (1955), 175–77; Edward Wasiolek, "Relativity in *Gulliver's Travels,"* PQ, 37 (1958), 110–16; and Helmut Papajewski, "Swift und Berkeley," *Anglia,* 78 (1959), 29–55.]

[12] *Revue de littérature comparée,* 4 (1924), 149–54.

[13] *JEGP,* 23 (1924), 460–62.

(1931),[14] an article distinguished as much for its thoroughness as for the restraint of its conclusions, traces almost all the disagreeable traits of the Yahoos to accounts of monkeys and savages in books of authentic travel by Dampier, Herbert, Wafer, and others. Placed alongside Gulliver's description of the Yahoos, the morbidly sensational passages in these accounts seem to out-Swift Swift in their disgustingness and filth. They are at the same time a striking contrast to descriptions of "noble savages" common in imaginary voyages and less frequent in accounts of authentic voyagers. While Frantz's study considerably strengthens Collins' claim for Swift's use of Herbert, its importance lies primarily in its demonstration of a general relationship between the authentic voyages and *Gulliver,* whose comedy derives partially from its elaborate pretense of authenticity.

A review of the major conclusions regarding Swift's sources up to 1932 appeared in Harold Williams' *Dean Swift's Library* (Cambridge, 1932), a valuable catalog and description of books owned by Swift, based on two manuscript lists, the original sale catalog (1745), and Williams' own extensive knowledge of Swiftiana. This volume was apparently in the press before account could be taken of Frantz's study on the voyagers, and it preceded by several years other important developments in source studies of *Gulliver.* Among these is Willard Bonner's useful book on the vogue of travel literature in the early eighteenth century, *Captain William Dampier: Buccaneer-Author* (Stanford, 1934). Dampier, whom Gulliver claims as a "cousin," was the foremost voyager and explorer of his time, the late seventeenth and early eighteenth centuries. His scrupulously kept journals, written often under severe hardship and, on at least one occasion, preserved for the eyes of civilization by being sealed in a bamboo cane, stimulated the unprecedented rage for travel books. Henry Beunting, a Grubstreet writer, exploited it by preparing a volume entitled *The Travels of the Holy Patriarchs, Prophets, Judges, Kings, Our Saviour Christ, and His Apostles, as They Are Related in the Old and New Testament: With a Description of the Towns and Places to Which They Travelled, and How Many English Miles They Stood from Jerusalem* (p. 62). The feverish preparation of travel books led some authors to curious shifts of composition. Authentic voyagers were not above heightening their material with flights of imagination. Pseudo-travellers were, of course, even more reliant upon imagination, when they weren't plagiarizing authentic accounts or the works of their fellows. Fraudulent travel accounts (a classic hoax in the history of England, George Psalmanazar's pose as a Formosan and his subsequent *Historical and Geographical Description of Formosa,* 1704, is a hoax which bears some relation to

Gulliver itself[15]) were welcomed by the eighteenth-century public, which, as Bonner points out, was "travel-crazy."

It was this taste and the ways it was met which Swift in his own way sought to exploit. There is abundant evidence that he was deeply read in travel literature. Bonner's chapter on Swift's relation to Dampier makes all the obvious connections, including Swift's use of Dampier's unceremonius, factual style, and his spoofing with Dampier's nautical jargon, a mode of literary borrowing which Davis has called "Swift's regular practice, something which varies between parody and imitation, and provides him with the roles of Bickerstaff, Drapier, and Gulliver," and in Dampier's case, "lends him the very speech of this plain, serious and honest seaman with eager curiosity and notable gift for veracity." [16]

Ricardo Quintana in *The Mind and Art of Jonathan Swift* (1936), glances sceptically, as did Williams, at the methods and results of the source study of *Gulliver* (pp. 296–303). His penetrating discussion clarifies and summarizes whatever of value had thus far emerged from this approach to Swift's work. He takes issue with Gilbert Chinard,[17] who saw a source for *Gulliver* in Baron de Lahontan's *Dialogues curieux entre l'auteur et un sauvage de bon sens qui a voyagé* (1702), a *libertin*, primitivist work. Quintana points out that the striking parallels which Chinard noted are merely superficial, for if Swift used Lahontan at all, "he took over from the *libertin* not the barest shadow of the latter's real meaning." In Lahontan, for instance, the gentle and virtuous savages attribute some of the evils of civilization to civilized man's use of salt. This is precisely the kind of environmentalist nonsense that would draw Swift's fire, and when he has Gulliver declare his own liberation from salt, claiming that he knew of "no Animal to be fond of it but Man" (IV, ii; HD, XI, 216), this manifest absurdity was meant to speak for itself. The technique here is, in Davis' words, "something . . . between imitation and parody," but we must take care not to regard it as mere imitation.

Because the voyage to Laputa, often called the least successful of the travels, resisted early attempts to discover its sources, some critics concluded that its weakness derived from Swift's having relied on personal idiosyncrasy instead of source material. This view became untenable when, in 1937, Marjorie Nicolson and Nora Mohler[18]

---

[15] The best discussion of Gulliver as imposter is James R. Wilson's "Swift's Alazon," *Studia neophilologica*, 30 (1958), 153–64.

[16] "Recent Studies of Swift: A Survey," *UTQ*, 7 (1938), 277.

[17] Ed., Baron de Lahontan's *Dialogues curieux*, 1931, pp. 60–62.

[18] "The Scientific Background of Swift's Voyage to Laputa," *Annals of Science*, 2 (1937), 299–334; "Swift's 'Flying Island' in the Voyage to Laputa," *Annals of Science*, 2 (1937), 405–30.

presented their remarkable discovery of Swift's use of the *Philosophical Transactions* and other publications of the Royal Society for all but two of the projects in the Grand Academy. Not a mere catalog of parallel passages, Nicolson and Mohler's article also deals with Swift's design and technique in appropriating, with peculiar fidelity, his source material: "For the most part, he simply set down before his readers experiments actually performed by members of the Royal Society, more preposterous to the layman than anything imagination could invent and more devastating in their satire because of their essential truth to source." Alterations, when present, extend at most to ridiculously combining two experiments or carrying an experiment "one step further—and the added step carries us over the precipice of nonsense" (p. 322).

In another article Nicolson and Mohler examine the derivation of the Flying Island. They find its origin, like that of the projects of the Grand Academy, in contemporary science, particularly in the dipping needle and terrella of William Gilbert. In addition to its part in the allegory of English-Irish relations, the Flying Island is a parody of the numerous and fantastic flying machines which appeared in the science fiction of Swift's day, the imaginary extra-terrestrial voyage. Of this genre Miss Nicolson has more to say in her admirable study, *Voyages to the Moon* (New York, 1948) which illuminates, among other things, Swift's relation to the genre.

R. W. Frantz returned to *Gulliver's* sources in 1938 with "Gulliver's 'Cousin Sympson,' " [19] in which he conclusively demonstrated Swift's use of a hitherto unnoticed source, *A New Voyage to the East Indies* (1715). Frantz suggested that "William Symson," the pretended author of this imaginary—and largely plagiarized—travel book may have had some connection with Gulliver's equally fictitious cousin, "Richard Sympson." The parallel passage noted by Frantz, evidently the source of Gulliver's description of Lilliputian and other writing habits, supersedes a less similar passage in *L'Histoire des Sévarambes* which Borkowsky had pointed out. Swift, as always, makes of his source something different if not wholly new: to the three kinds of writing described in Symson, including the predecessor of "aslant from one Corner of the Paper to the other, like Ladies in England," Swift adds yet another method, "from down to up," solemnly ascribed to "the Cascagians" (I, vi; HD, XI, 41).

In 1941 John R. Moore[20] argued for yet another *libertin* voyage as a source for *Gulliver*, Tyssot de Patot's *Voyages et aventures de Jacques Massé* (1710), and in doing so challenged Eddy's assertion that indi-

---

[19] *HLQ*, 1 (1938), 329–34.
[20] "A New Source for *Gulliver's Travels*," *SP*, 38 (1941), 66–80.

vidually the realistic imaginary voyages, of which Tyssot's is an example, had no significance as forerunners of *Gulliver*, since "no direct relation to any of them can be traced" (Eddy, p. 29). Moore notes a great many resemblances, none very convincing, such as Massé's and Gulliver's both being ship's surgeons, Swift's and Tyssot's disapprobation of war, fire-fighting in Swift and Tyssot (in both, alarms are sounded and ladders are used), and the presence in Tyssot of a strange animal which appears to be a cross between a Houyhnhnm and a Yahoo. Moore recognizes that Swift and Tyssot were philosophically uncongenial, but except for his comment that the conclusion of Gulliver's exploit as fireman seems an "almost conscious burlesque" of a corresponding passage in *Massé*, Moore leaves unexplored whatever tactical relation Gulliver might have to *Massé*.

The last two decades have seen a falling off of source studies on *Gulliver*, perhaps in part because of the feeling that the task is essentially completed, and in part because of an awareness, reflected in the studies of Nicolson and Mohler, Bonner, and Frantz, that Swift's satire can best be understood when placed against broad traditions rather than particular works. While there is a great deal of the topical and the particular in *Gulliver's Travels*, its literary satire, no less than its political, is by no means limited to isolated skirmishes.

Somewhat outside the main stream of source studies is Margaret R. Grennan's exploration of Swift's possible use of Irish folklore in the first two voyages, "Lilliput and Leprecan: Gulliver and the Irish Tradition" (1945).[21] Unsympathetic to suggestions that the Lilliputians are related to Ctesius' "horrible grubs" and to the pygmies, Miss Grennan seeks to trace their "charm" and "humanity" to the Irish leprechaun tradition. Miss Grennan, aware of the obvious objections to her argument, claims that Lilliput "owes much of its charm to Swift's partial surrender to a spirit not entirely his own," that "perhaps, in spite of himself, the native speech went deep into the unwilling consciousness of the Dean," and that these uncongenial elements were "retained by a disapproving but retentive memory." This is as close to invoking "the deep well of unconscious cerebration" as Swift source-seeking has ever come.

The direction of Miss Grennan's work indicates, perhaps, that students of Swift's sources have taken to heart Harold Williams' caveat to "the restless discoverer of source books" whose "eager search in hidden corners for similarities of phrase or narrative may easily become a mistaken pastime." How easily we have already seen. Our knowledge of Swift's use of Sturmy, for instance, welcome though it may be, does not alter the value, aptness, and perspicuity of Scott's

[21] *ELH*, 12 (1945), 188–202.

note on the passage ("This is a parody upon the accounts of storms
and naval manoeuvres frequent in old voyages and is merely an as-
semblage of sea terms, put together at random.")—written a half-
century before Knowles's discovery—a note which remains its best
comment.[22] Nonetheless, a proper understanding of Swift's literary
relationships tells us a great deal about the intent and character of
the satire, its relation to its traditions, and, in the fullest Aristotelian
sense, its nature.

[22] *Works of Swift*, 1814, xii, 108.

On the Philosophical Background of
Gulliver's Travels

by T. O. Wedel

Swift, the master of irony among the moderns, has achieved no greater ironic masterpiece than the posthumous reputation of *Gulliver's Travels*. Written to vex the world, not to divert it, hiding within its cloak of wit and romantic invention the savage indignation of a lifetime, the fiercest indictment of the pride of man yet penned in our language, it has become, forsooth, a children's book—an example, so Goethe thought, of the failure of allegory to make an idea prevail.[1] "Types and Fables," so runs a passage in *The Tale of a Tub*[2] which could be applied prophetically to *Gulliver's Travels*,—

> the writing having been perhaps more careful and curious in adorning, than was altogether necessary, it has fared with these Vehicles after the usual Fate of Coaches, over-finely painted and gilt; that the transitory Gazers have so dazzled their Eyes, and fill'd their Imaginations with the outward lustre, as neither to regard or consider the Person or the Parts of the Owner within.

The failure of posterity to appreciate the philosophical thesis of Gulliver's travels, is not, however, due solely to the triumph of Swift's art. The year of our Lord 1726, when Gulliver appeared, was in no mood to put a proper value upon a work which spoke of *homo sapiens* as "the most pernicious race of little odious vermin that nature ever suffered to crawl upon the surface of the earth." We need only remind ourselves that the very year previous there had appeared, in Swift's own Dublin, Hutcheson's first panegyric essay[3] on the soundness of

---

"On the Philosophical Background of Gulliver's Travels*" by T. O. Wedel. From* Studies in Philology, *23 (1926), 434–50.*

[1] Goethe, *Werke,* Weimar, 1901, XL, 220.

[2] *Tale of a Tub,* ed. Guthkelch, Oxford, 1920, p. 66.

[3] As republished in 1726, Hutcheson's two first essays bore the titles: *Inquiry concerning Beauty, Order, Harmony, and Design,* and *Inquiry concerning Moral Good and Evil.*

man's benevolent instincts, a classic expression for the century of the
new optimistic creed, and itself the resultant of a respectable tradition.
No, neither the eighteenth century nor the nineteenth has expressed
anything but scorn for the view of man to be found in *Gulliver's
Travels*. Eighteenth century criticism, in fact, is remarkably silent
about Swift. Yet when *Gulliver's Travels* is discussed by Orrery, Warton, Young, Jeffrey, or Scott, its philosophy is referred to as the result
of a diseased mind, blaspheming as it does a nature little lower than
that of the angels.[4] "In what ordure," exclaims Young in his *Conjectures*,[5] "hast thou dipped thy pencil! What a monster hast thou
made of the 'Human face divine!'" The German Herder, to be sure,
attempts to appreciate Swift's misanthropy, at the same time preserving
his constant enthusiasm for Shaftesbury. But it is John Wesley who,
alone among eighteenth century readers, can cite the Voyage to the
Houyhnhnms with real enthusiasm. In his longest written work, *The
Doctrine of Original Sin*,[6] it is Swift rather than St. Augustine upon
whom he leans for quotations.

Yet if Swift had written *Gulliver's Travels* a few generations earlier,
he would have given little cause for complaint. Pascal would have
understood him, as would La Rochefoucauld and Boileau;[7] so would
Montaigne; so would Bayle. For the transition from the seventeenth
century to the eighteenth was experiencing a revolution in ethical
thought. "Rarely, if ever," says Brunetière,[8] with perhaps too dogmatic
assurance, "has so profound a transformation occurred more swiftly.
Everything has changed." The pessimism of Pascal has given way to

---

[4] "In this last part of his imaginary travels," says Orrery (*Remarks on the Life
and Writings of Dr. Jonathan Swift*, Letter 15), "Swift has indulged a misanthropy
that is intolerable. The representation which he has given us of human nature, must
terrify and even debase the mind of the reader who views it." Walter Scott in his
preface to *Gulliver* is no less severe:

> The voyage to the land of the Houyhnhnms is, beyond contest, the basest
> and most unworthy part of the work. It holds mankind forth in a light too
> degrading for contemplation, and which, if admitted, would justify or palliate
> the worst vices, by exhibiting them as natural attributes, and rendering reforma-
> tion from a state of such depravity a task too desperate to be attempted.

Jeffrey's comment (*Edinburgh Review*, Sept., 1816) is: "The scope of the whole
work, and indeed of all his writings is to degrade and villify human nature."
A typical modern comment is that of Courthope (*Liberal Movement in English
Literature*, London, 1885, p. 112): "Chivalrous feeling could scarcely breathe in
the same atmosphere as Gulliver."

[5] Steinke, M. W., *Edward Young's Conjectures on Original Composition*, New York,
1913, p. 59.

[6] *The Doctrine of Original Sin* was written in 1757.

[7] Boileau's eighth Satire constitutes, together with Montaigne's *Apologie de
Raymond Sébonde*, perhaps the best parallel to Swift's picture of man as beast.

[8] Brunetière's article on Bayle (*Études Critiques*, v, 116).

the optimism of Leibnitz; the theory of self-love of La Rochefoucauld to the theory of benevolence of Hutcheson and Hume; the scepticism of Montaigne to the rationalism of Locke, Toland, and Clarke; the dualism of Nature and Grace to a monistic inclusion of Nature under the rule of a beneficent God; the bold warfare between atheism and faith to a mere gentlemen's quarrel between revealed and natural religion. In fact, it is this revolutionary background which alone can explain Swift's purpose in writing *Gulliver's Travels.*

Swift's darker meaning, to be sure, does not lie on the surface, for, as Johnson noted in his biographical sketch, he was the most reticent of men. Rarely does he reveal his opinions or his feelings without a cloak of irony; rarely does he quote an author. Indeed an article of his artistic creed discouraged quotation.[9] Pedantry is absent from his writings to a fault. While Bolingbroke, in the famous correspondence, overloads his page with learning, Swift turns out epigrams on Ireland or the weather. *Vive la bagatelle* was his motto. He might illustrate the saying of Joubert: "The wise man is serious about few things." Or he might have applied to himself his own maxim:[10] "Some people take more care to hide their wisdom than their folly."

Yet the student of Swift is not left entirely without guidance as to his philosophical opinions. The *Tale of a Tub,* for example, furnishes plentiful evidence of his distrust of metaphysics on the one hand, of his hatred of mystical enthusiasm on the other. A stray remark in his *Letter to a Young Clergyman* tells us that he did not approve of Locke's attack upon innate ideas. His *Sermon on the Trinity,* thought by Wesley to be one of the great sermons of the age, helps, when read in the light of contemporary thought, to define the same anti-rationalism which appears in *Gulliver's Travels* and which animated his attacks upon the Deists. The *Sermon on Conscience,* in turn, defending religion against the upholders of mere moral honesty and honour, reads like a rebuttal of both Shaftesbury and Mandeville. The *Correspondence* yields more than one hint that Swift felt himself to be on the side of the opposition with reference to the growing optimism of Pope and Bolingbroke. In two letters, in particular, Swift plays the truant to his creed of reticence, giving us in round terms his formula of misanthropy. I shall quote the respective passages in full. The first, indeed, constitutes the *locus classicus* for the critic of Gulliver.[11]

> I have ever hated all nations, professions, and communities, and all my love is toward individuals: for instance, I hate the tribe of lawyers,

[9] See his *Letter to a Young Clergyman* (*Prose Works,* ed. Temple Scott, London, 1909, III, 211).

[10] *Thoughts on Various Subjects* (*Prose Works,* I, 278).

[11] Swift's *Correspondence,* ed. Ball, London, 1910–13, III, 276.

but I love Counsellor Such-a-one, and Judge Such a-one. . . . But principally I hate and detest that animal called man, although I heartily love John, Peter, Thomas, and so forth. This is the system upon which I have governed myself many years, but do not tell, and so I shall go on till I have done with them. I have got materials toward a treatise, proving the falsity of that definition *animal rationale,* and to show it would be only *rationis capax.* Upon this great foundation of misanthropy, though not in Timon's manner, the whole building of my Travels is erected; and I will never have peace of mind till all honest men are of my opinion.

In the second and later letter[12] Swift is dissuading Pope from undertaking a refutation of La Rochefoucauld, who, Swift says, "is my favourite, because I found my whole character in him." "I desire you and all my friends will take a special care that my disaffection to the world may not be imputed to my age, for I have credible witnesses ready to depose that it has never varied from the twenty-first to the fifty-eighth year of my life. . . . I tell you after all, that I do not hate mankind: it is *vous autres* who hate them, because you would have them reasonable animals, and are angry for being disappointed."

Finally, besides all such incidental aids for the critic, we have *Gulliver's Travels* itself—its views on education and politics; its attack on science; its satire on luxury, war, and commerce, bordering on a kind of primitivism; its dualism of Yahoos and Houyhnhnms; above all, its savage indignation at the animalism and pettiness of man, culminating in its magnificent peroration on pride.

And in trying to interpret in the light of the ethical revolution of his day, at least some of this provocative satire, I may begin with his misanthropic view in general, his hatred of the animal called man, his love for individuals—"a sentiment," so Thomas Warton thought,[13] voicing the general opinion of posterity, "that dishonors him as a man, a Christian, and a philosopher." A hard view of man it is, clearly, yet no more severe than that of the seventeenth century as a whole. Parallels to Swift's very words can be found several times over. Listen, for example to Pascal:[14]

> The nature of man may be viewed in two ways: the one according to its end, and then he is great and incomparable; the other, according to the multitude, just as we judge of the nature of the horse and the dog, popularly, . . . and then man is abject and vile. . . . The nature of man is wholly natural, *omne animal.*

Or to a similar judgment of La Bruyère:[15] "A reasonable man may

[12] *Correspondence,* III, 292.
[13] See Pope's *Works,* ed. Elwin and Courthope, VII, 53.
[14] Pascal, *Thoughts* (tr. Temple Classics), Nos. 415, 94.
[15] La Bruyère, *Caractères,* chap. "De l'homme."

hate mankind in general; he discovers in it so little of virtue. But he is ready to excuse the individual . . . and strives to deserve as little as possible a similar indulgence." One is tempted to quote by way of contrast Hazlitt's confession,[16] equally typical of more recent centuries: "I believe in the theoretical benevolence, but the practical malignity of man."

In more general form, Swift's hard view of man could be duplicated scores of times even without resorting to the Ancients, the Fathers, or the Calvinists. Although, as we shall see, a more flattering doctrine had already appeared early in the seventeenth century, his is after all the prevailing judgment on human nature from Montaigne to Locke, among men of the world as well as ascetic Christians. Even Bayle at the turn of the new century, arch sceptic that he was, still clings to it. His article on Ovid, for example, in the *Dictionnaire,* quoting voluminously from Cicero and St. Augustine to Esprit and the Moderns, reads like a pedantic prospectus of *Gulliver's Travels.* In Bayle's view, man is still an ungovernable animal, ruled by self-love, given over to evil incomparably more than to good, the slight glimmering of reason which has been left him usually worsted in the fight against the passions, his only hope, apart from utilitarian virtue, being divine grace. Vauvenargues, a moralist writing in the middle of the eighteenth century, may well exclaim:[17] "Man is at present in disgrace among all those who think; they heap upon him all manner of vices." Only he adds: "Perhaps he is soon to awake and to demand the restitution of his virtues." By the year 1726, in England at least, the restitution of man's virtues was already well under way. The dignity of human nature is already on everyone's lips. Locke and the Deists had given man a new trust in Reason; the Cambridge Platonists and Shaftesbury were discovering in him a moral sense, even in the hitherto despised realm of the passions. Nothing seems more certain to the new age than the existence of a beneficent deity, and the consequent goodness of his creation. Optimistic theodicies are being written on all sides,[18] explaining away the evil from this best of all possible worlds. "Place the mind in its right posture," declares a Spectator paper,[19] "it will immediately discover its innate propension to beneficence. Persons conscious of their own integrity, satisfied with themselves and

---

[16] Hazlitt, *Aphorisms on Man,* No. 46 (*Works,* ed. Waller and Glover, London, 1904–06, XII, 222).

[17] Sainte-Beuve's article on Vauvenargues in the *Causeries du Lundi,* November 18, 1850.

[18] Optimism is almost full-blown in Henry More's *Divine Dialogues* (1668). The *De Origine Mali* of William King, Swift's ecclesiastical superior, appeared in 1702; the *Théodicée* of Leibnitz, in 1710.

[19] *Spectator,* No. 610.

their condition, and full of confidence in a Supreme Being, and the hope of immortality, survey all about them with a flow of goodwill. As trees which like their soil, they shoot out in expressions of kindness and bend beneath their own precious load, to the hand of the gatherer." A popular article in the *Gentleman's Magazine*[20] (1732) sets out to prove "that men are as generally good, as they are represented bad." Any other conclusion is declared to be a blasphemy against God; "for neither God nor man can be good but by their works."

Definitions of vice and virtue are at sixes and sevens. Evil and good, once set over against each other as equivalent to Nature and Grace, now oppose each other within the natural realm alone. Pride has become a virtue. When Pope proposed to refute La Rochefoucauld by dissolving vices into virtues, as the cynic of the seventeenth century had dissolved virtues into vices, he set himself a supernumerary task. The thing was being done all around him. An unworldly definition of virtue had become almost unintelligible. Tindal, the Deist, asserts that the Sermon on the Mount is absurd for practical life.[21] "Pascal and La Rochefoucauld," says Voltaire,[22] "who were read by everyone, have accustomed the French public to interpret the word self-love always in a bad sense. Only in the eighteenth century did a change come about, so that the ideas of vice and pride were no longer necessarily attached to the word." Precisely so. Mandeville gained a stormy hearing for his paradox of "private vices, public benefits" simply because at least half of his terminology was being dropped from the new vocabulary.

In theological terms, what was happening of course was the avowed or tacit denial of the doctrine of original sin. Human nature was being absolved of corruption. The ancient Christian faith, in the words of Pascal, had rested on but two things, "the corruption of nature and redemption by Jesus Christ." Half at least of Pascal's formula is seldom spoken of after 1700. Even before that date optimism and orthodoxy jostle each other in unexpected places. Jeremy Taylor[23] is already suspected of unorthodoxy on the subject of original sin. Tillotson, though he bows to the traditional dogma,[24] became for the Deists a favorite prop for their rationalistic doctrines. A popular version of both the old and the new in theological thought is Bishop Burnet's naïve account (1680) of the death of the Earl of Rochester.

---

[20] *Gentleman's Magazine,* Jan. and June, 1732.
[21] Tindal, *Christianity as Old as the Creation,* London, 1732, p. 312.
[22] *Encyclopédie,* article "Intérêt."
[23] Swift's *Prose Works,* III, 176.
[24] See, for example, Tillotson's Sermon, *On the Goodness of God* (*Wórks,* 10 vols., London, 1820, Sermon No. 145).

Though Rochester's views can lay no claim to consistency, he is at least an optimist. Man's instincts must be restrained here and there perhaps, but they are not evil. The story of Adam's fall is absurd— one man cheating the whole world. The honest Bishop offers no rational explanation; he merely asserts[25] in the name of Platonism and Augustinian Christianity that "common experience tells us there is a great disorder in our Nature, which is not easily rectified: all philosophers were sensible of it, and every man that designs to govern himself by Reason, feels the struggle between it and Nature. So that it is plain there is a lapse of the high powers of the Soul."

With the turn of the century, however, words like these are rarely heard. If anyone doubts that by the year 1700 a new philosophy was in the air, he need merely read a designedly orthodox work such as Locke's *Reasonableness of Christianity.* Christianity is no longer for Locke, what it was for Pascal, a healer of souls, but a supernatural blunderbuss enforcing the police regulations of natural morality. Adam's fall, so Locke argues, brought the punishment of death upon the world, but implies no corruption of nature. "If by death, threatened to Adam, were meant the corruption of human nature in his posterity, 'tis strange that the New Testament should not anywhere take notice of it." [26] Locke's literalism is indeed daring in view of centuries of Pauline theology. And while occasionally a writer on divinity saw that here lay the chief danger to the old orthodoxy in Locke's appealing philosophy, the prevailing thought of the century passed on to other issues, busying itself with asserting the necessity of revelation for natural law, or, in Samuel Johnson's phrase, defending the apostles against the charge of forgery once a week. Wesley, harking back to pagan antiquity for parallels to his own unflattering view of man, and glancing at the new gospel, exclaims: "But how much more knowing than these old pagans are the present generation of Christians! How many laboured panegyrics do we now read and hear on the dignity of human nature!" . . . "I cannot see that we have much need of Christianity. Nay, not any at all; for 'they that are whole have no need of a physician!' . . . Nor can Christian philosophy, whatever be thought of the pagan, be more properly defined than in Plato's words: 'the only true method of healing a distempered soul.' But what need of this if we are in perfect health?" [27] And in

[25] Burnet, G., *Some Passages of the Life and Death of the Right Honorable John, Earl of Rochester,* London, 1680, p. 85.

[26] Locke, *The Reasonableness of Christianity as delivered in the Scriptures,* London, 1695, p. 7.

[27] See Sermon 127, *The Deceitfulness of the Human Heart; The Doctrine of Original Sin* (Wesley, *Works,* New York, 1832, v, 510 ff.).

refutation of contemporary optimism Wesley proceeds to unload upon
the reader page upon page of *Gulliver*.

In the world of political thought, the clash between old and new is
perhaps nowhere so concretely exhibited as in the contrasting theories
regarding the state of nature. For not in *Gulliver* only are Yahoos
set over against Houyhnhnms. In fact it looks like too simple a
discovery to point out that in the last voyage of the *Travels* we have,
designedly or not, Hobbes contrasted with Locke. And yet the parallel
holds good surprisingly well. Men in Hobbes' state of nature, like
Swift's Yahoos, are "in that condition which is called war; and such a
war, as is of every man against every man . . . with no arts, no letters,
no society, and, which is worst of all, continual fear of violent danger;
and the life of man, solitary, poor, nasty, brutish, and short." [28] And
while Hobbes' brevity of description with regard to his state of war pre-
vents elaboration of the parallel, the corresponding similarity between
Locke and Swift is certainly tempting. Men in Locke's state of nature,
like the Houyhnhnms, are rational creatures, "living together according to reason, without a common superior,"—in a state of liberty
without license, every one administering the laws of nature for himself, laws of temperance and mutual benevolence.[29] The relation of
Swift to Hobbes and to Locke is a subject for separate investigation.
On the whole, I think (and Swift's political writings would furnish
evidence in abundance), he stands nearer to Hobbes. In *Gulliver's
Travels*, however, Swift is clearly neither Hobbes nor Locke. Gulliver
is neither Yahoo nor Houyhnhnm. He cannot attain to the rational
felicity of the Houyhnhnms. Neither has he sunk to the level of the
Yahoos, though this is a doubtful advantage. He lacks the strength
of a healthy animal, and his glimmering of reason has unhappily
burdened him with responsibility of conscience.

Indeed, if Swift's own hints regarding the meaning of his book
are heeded, it is in the contrast between Yahoo and Houyhnhnm
that his main thesis lies hid. Gulliver, occupying a position between
the two, part beast, part reason, is Swift's allegorical picture of the
dual nature of man. He is not Houyhnhnm, *animal rationale*, nor is
he Yahoo. He is *rationis capax*. One could apply to *Gulliver's Travels*
a passage of Cicero, quoted with approval by both St. Augustine and
Bayle: "Nature has been to man not a mother, but a step-mother—
sending him into the world naked, frail, and infirm, toiling under a
burden of care, fearful, slothful, and given over to lust, but not without a spark of divine reason." [30]

---

[28] Hobbes, *Leviathan*, Part I, chap. 13.
[29] Locke, *Two Treatises on Government*, Book II, Chaps. 2, 3.
[30] Bayle, *Dictionnaire*, article "Ovid," Remark E.

Animal rationale—animal rationis capax! Swift's somewhat scholastic distinction turns out, in the light of seventeenth century thought, to be by no means scholastic. It symbolizes, in fact, the chief intellectual battle of the age. Swift seems to have seen clearly enough that in assaulting man's pride in reason, he was attacking the new optimism at its very root. His enmity to rationalistic dogmatising was the one enduring intellectual passion of his life. It animates his orthodoxy in his sermon on the Trinity; it prompts the dangerous laughter of *The Tale of a Tub;* it explains his merciless satire of the Deists.

The phrase *animal rationale* can be traced at least as far back as Seneca[31] and ancient Stoicism. This fact alone explains much. For it is precisely the circle of ideas represented by Stoicism, however changed in form through centuries of filtration, which the seventeenth century, like the fifth, was still finding it difficult to assimilate. Stoicism has ever been associated with optimism. It is the Stoic who worships pride. And despite the noble appeal of its ethical heroism,— or perhaps one had better say because of it—Stoicism has constituted one of Christianity's gravest dangers. *Corruptio optimi pessima est.* No Christian in the Augustinian sense could have said with Epictetus: "I was never hindered in my will or compelled against my wish. . . . Who can hinder me against my own judgments, or put compulsion on me? I am as safe as Zeus." [32] The Stoic faith in a beneficent deity and a rational world robbed the universe of evil. To follow nature was to obey God and reason. The wise man, to be sure, had to conquer his passions; but the passions themselves were merely wrong opinion. The Stoic was still master of his fate.

It was Stoicism in the form of the Pelagian heresy against which St. Augustine threw the whole weight of his eloquence in the last great doctrinal war of his career. Man for Pelagius, too, was not by nature evil. "For they think," so St. Augustine defines the belief of his enemies, "that, by the strength of their own will, they will fulfill the commands of the law; and wrapped up in their pride, they are not converted to assisting grace." [33] Conceive of God as goodness and benevolence, of nature as His creation, include man in nature, let the myth of the Fall imply, as it did for Locke, merely a legal death penalty laid upon otherwise innocent descendants of Adam, who are rational beings, free to choose good and evil, and you have the Pelagian heresy.

---

[31] Seneca, *Epist.,* 41, 8.
[32] Epictetus, *Discourses,* IV, 1. 12.
[33] Augustine, *Anti-Pelagian Writings (Nicene and Post-Nicene Fathers,* ed. Schaff, New York, 1902), p. 412.

Of the popularity of Stoicism in this period there can be no doubt. According to Strowski,[34] the author oftenest reprinted in the first half of the seventeenth century was Du Vair, whose *Philosophie Morale des Stoïques* was one of the chief Stoic texts, together with a similar compendium of Justus Lipsius. Coming to the fore by way of translation and paraphrase, Stoicism, as I shall try to show a little later, soon suffered a sea-change, and was destined, in its new form, to conquer the world. For the moment, however, its victory was delayed, though the warfare against it was confused, and though many a skirmish was fought on secondary issues. The passions, for one thing, found defenders against the Stoic attitude of disdain. Positivistic observers of man simply denied that man was ruled by reason. Balzac[35] ridicules the Stoics as "that inhuman sect which, in cutting off from man his passions and his feelings, desires to rob him of half of himself. In place of having created a wise man, the Stoics have merely created a statue." Or as Swift himself puts it in one of his maxims: "The Stoical scheme of supplying our wants by lopping off our desires is like cutting off our feet, when we want shoes." [36] La Rochefoucauld, man of the world, sees human nature as merely the dupe of the ruling passion of self-love. As the century advances, optimism itself takes to throwing stones at the Stoics, actually defending the passions as good in themselves. Sénault writes a treatise[37] proving the Stoic wise man a fiction and the passions useful in the moral life. A similar defense is found in the *Enchiridion Ethicum* of the Cambridge Platonist, Henry More. The Augustinian tradition, of course, is against the Stoics. Jansen's *Augustinus* is an attack upon them; so is Arnauld's *Fréquente Communion.*[38] And Pascal, dualist always, accepts neither the man of the world's cynical acceptance of man as a creature of the passions, nor the Stoic's pride in having conquered them. It is he who expresses the conviction of the mystic: "The heart has its reasons, which the reason knows not of." [39] Machiavellians, Epicureans, and Christians are at one in laughing at the Stoic's vain pretensions that the passions can be conquered, and that the will is free.

Combatants of divergent loyalties again united in attacking Stoic rationalism itself—Montaigne, Bayle, Pascal: Epicurean, sceptic, and Christian. Montaigne indeed may be said to be all three in one. And to understand Swift's own position, Montaigne is of particular importance. The best commentary on *Gulliver's Travels* is the great

[34] Strowski, *Pascal et son Temps,* 1907, I, 106.

[35] Strowski, *op. cit.,* I, 104.

[36] Swift, *Thoughts on Various Subjects (Prose Works,* I, 277).

[37] Sénault, *De l'Usage des Passions,* Paris, 1641.

[38] Strowski, *op. cit.,* I, 124.

[39] Pascal, *Thoughts* (Temple Classics), No. 277.

Apologie de Raymond Sébonde. According to Busson's recent study of rationalism in the Renaissance, Montaigne sums up in popular form the scepticism of the preceding centuries of enlightenment. Now the rationalism of the Renaissance differed from that of the eighteenth century precisely in that it was a sceptical balancing of reason against faith, including reason itself among the objects of doubt. *Que sais je?* asks Montaigne. What do I know? Montaigne's *Apologie*, like *Gulliver's Travels,* is a scathing attack upon Stoic pride. Man is placed on a level almost lower than that of the dog and the horse. In fact Montaigne's primitivism, imitated by Swift—his disgust with the pompous boasts of civilization—is a good deal softened in *Gulliver's Travels*. . . .

But by the time that Swift wrote his own treatise to vex the world, scepticism and the belief in the corruption of human nature had given way to rationalism and an optimistic faith in man. The Stoic creed had suffered its sea-change. Sceptic, Epicurean, dualistic Christian had surrendered.

And the founder of the new faith was no other than the father of modern philosophy, Descartes himself. To the layman, burrowing his way into the history of ideas in the seventeenth century, it is almost disconcerting to discover how all roads lead to the author of the *Discourse on Method*. Let any one, after reading Montaigne's *Apologie,* turn to Descartes' treatise on the passions and a new planet swims into his ken. For the first assumption of Descartes is precisely the Stoic faith in a beneficent God and an uncorrupted nature. A good God cannot deceive us, and our reason is from God; hence our reason is to be trusted. And while the Stoicism of Epictetus still left within man a dualism of reason and passion, this, too, is obliterated by Descartes. The passions become good. *Elles sont toutes bonnes*. Vicious and evil instincts are denied the name of passions—ingratitude, impudence, effrontery. Reversing the method of La Rochefoucauld, Descartes dissolves a bad passion into that good one which nearly resembles it. Envy, for example, becomes a praiseworthy love of distributive justice. Pride is good, except when wrongly applied. Humility is scored as evil when it persuades us that we are feeble or unable to exercise our free will. Descartes' treatise on the passions does not, of course, yet picture the man of sentiment of Vauvenargues, or Rousseau; man is still decidedly *animal rationale,* master over himself like the heroes of Corneille:

> Je suis, maître du moi, comme de l'univers;
> Je le suis, je veux l'être.

But one may perhaps already see the eighteenth century in the offing —Deism, Shaftesbury, even the new anti-rationalism of Rousseau.

Though Cartesianism, as we have seen, found plentiful enemies in the seventeenth century, its ultimate victory was a foregone conclusion. It became for a time the ally of orthodoxy itself. Deceived by the first-fruits of the Cartesian method, resulting as it did in a dogmatic faith in God and immortality, the Church, fifty years later, discovered that she had fallen victim to seduction. The Deism of Toland, for example, is almost pure Descartes. Eighteenth century orthodoxy, itself turned rationalist and optimist, found no weapons adequate to fight the Deists. Swift was one of few bold enough to oppose them squarely with an appeal to the weakness of human reason. Bossuet still saw the danger, as did the light-hearted Bayle.[40] And Pascal rested his dualism precisely on the necessity of reconciling Montaigne and Descartes. Nowhere, perhaps, is the issue fought out in the seventeenth century more clearly expressed than in Pascal's little dialogue between himself and M. de Saci, in which Montaigne is set over against Epictetus—Montaigne, for whom man was on a level with the beasts; Epictetus (Descartes), for whom man was a god.

Clearly Swift belongs with Montaigne, La Rochefoucauld, and Bayle, among those who see man without illusion. But can he also be said to be a disciple of Pascal, the Christian? I do not think so. He did not, like Montaigne, achieve Epicurean tranquillity. He was decidedly not at ease in his inn. Neither could he feel kinship with the saints as could Pascal. Swift was not a mystic. One might apply to *Gulliver's Travels* Pascal's words: "It is dangerous to make man see too clearly his equality with the brutes, without showing him his greatness." [41] Even Swift's Utopia is the Utopia of Locke, not Plato's philosopher's kingdom, nor St. Augustine's City of God. He was a rationalist with no faith in reason. Against the language of the heart he harbored an almost Freudian complex. Wesley, we may be sure, would have found him strange company. Sceptic and misanthrope, Swift fell back upon *saeva indignatio* and the established religion of his country.

Yet Swift's view of man, as Wesley perceived, and as Professor Bernbaum[42] has pointed out in our own time, is essentially the view of the classical and Christian tradition. Almost any fair definition of that tradition would absolve *Gulliver's Travels* from the charge of being an isolated example of misanthropy.

[40] Bayle, *Dictionnaire*, article "Hobbes," Remark **E.**
[41] Pascal, *Thoughts* (Temple Classics), No. 418.
[42] *Gulliver's Travels*, ed. Bernbaum, New York, 1920, pp. x–xii.

Swift's Satire of the Second Person

by Henry W. Sams

In the Preface to *A Tale of a Tub* Swift observes that satire seldom scores an acknowledged hit. Every man is quick to understand the depravities of others, but he is obtuse concerning his own. He does not answer the satirist's accusation with confession. In fact, he is not aware that he may be the person to whom the accusation is addressed.

> You may preach in *Covent-Garden* against Foppery and Fornication, and *something else:* Against Pride, and Dissimulation, and Bribery, at *White Hall:* You may expose Rapine and Injustice in the *Inns* of *Court* Chapell: And in a *City* Pulpit be as fierce as you please, against Avarice, Hypocrisie and Extortion. 'Tis but a *Ball* bandied to and fro, and every Man carries a *Racket* about him to strike it from himself among the rest of the Company.

As a logical consequence of this observation Swift professed his intention to abjure satire, and to write instead a *Panegyrick upon the World,* with a second part to be entitled a *Modest Defense of the Proceedings of the Rabble in all Ages.*

Despite the fact that Swift's remark is made among ironies, it has a certain plausibility. Others have made similar comments. William Wotton, in his *Observations,* says that men who are ridiculed, if they deserve ridicule, "ought to sit down quietly under it." But common experience is that they do not do so. Far from sitting down quietly under it, men behave precisely as Swift says they do; they appropriate the witticism and apply it to someone else. "*Satyr is a sort of Glass,* wherein Beholders do generally discover every body's Face but their Own. . . ." [1]

The fact that Swift questioned the efficacy of satire, and yet practiced it, poses a dilemma of more than ironic force. It is a true problem. What Swift's resolution of it may have been is a matter worth serious examination.

"*Swift's Satire of the Second Person*" by Henry W. Sams. From English Literary History 26 (*1959*), *36–44*. Copyright © *1959* by the Johns Hopkins Press. Reprinted by permission of the Johns Hopkins Press.

[1] [Preface to *The Battle of the Books.*]

Some aspects of this question are very easily answered. Satire expressly aimed at a public personage usually scores. Readers readily join with Swift in his attacks upon Walpole, Warburton, Nottingham, and the rest of his list of enemies.

From the point of view of a twentieth-century reader of Swift, the satire most easily and immediately comprehended is that which chooses for its victim an individual remembered in history. Somewhat more difficult is the satire which attacks classes of persons. For example, the "Moderns" provide at best an academic butt for satire. A satisfying way to treat them is to think of them in the persons of Bentley and Wotton, or, more expansively, in the philosophical and scientific doctrines of the seventeenth century. By so doing the critic can anchor the satire firmly to persons and opinions remote in history.

This impulse of the modern reader is an indication of one element of Swift's extraordinary skill in rhetoric. One of the prerequisites of successful rhetoric is the creation of a cooperative relationship between speaker and audience. Ethos and pathos are crucial ingredients of persuasion. The exordium which succeeds in commending the speaker to his hearers must create a tacit alliance, and it is as an ally of the audience that the skilful speaker addresses himself to his argument.

Readers of Swift accept alliance. They join him in his attacks upon Walpole and upon the Moderns. Their readiness to join him assures his success against historical personages.

But the rhetorical alliance is operative only in satire of the third person. And if there be any truth in the observation which we have extracted from its context in the Preface to *A Tale of a Tub,* if it be of any real concern to Swift that every man carries with him a racket to bandy satire off upon his neighbors, Swift must at times have sought to violate this alliance, or to use it disingenuously.

Let us suppose that at times the butt of Swift's satire may be his reader. On this assumption we may undertake to trace the manner in which he circumvents the rhetorical alliance. This is the way to an anatomy of what we here call the "satire of the second person." Perhaps it may be a way to some insight into satiric art itself.

Considered in this light, Swift's frequent use of the device of putative authorship assumes a special significance, for it implies that his exordia may be ironic. From the very outset he holds himself aloof from the reader, commending not himself, but an intermediary buffoon. Many students of Swift have commented on this aspect of Swift's art. Its fundamental importance is everywhere noted. No other device so nearly comprehends within itself the qualities which distinguish the satires of Swift from direct criticism of the sort that one finds, for example, in the speeches of Burke.

In one sense, the effect of putative authorship may have been overestimated, for readers have sometimes assumed that the putative author introduced at the beginning of a work is a consistent character and that he remains the same throughout the work. As a matter of fact, the first function of the putative author is that of establishing a contract with the audience, that is, of the exordium. This function once fulfilled, the putative procedure may be only casually or occasionally remembered. Something of this sort occurs in *A Tale of a Tub*. To read the "Digression on Madness" as specifically attributable to the fictitious author of the dedication to Prince Posterity is an error. On the other hand, in the *Travels*, Gulliver is at once the author and the protagonist of his narrative. Readers are invited to accept a degree of what is called "identification" with him, and some readers, accepting this identification, have been inclined to take the fourth book of the *Travels* at literal face value, as a sermon instead of a satire.

Swift's exordia, his introductory contracts with his readers, are subtile, reassuring, and ambiguous. Their effect is to win approval and confidence even though they withhold the commitment of the controlling intelligence, that is, of Swift's own intelligence. They leave open the possibility that he may re-enter the argument when he finds re-entry expedient, and that he may re-enter as either enemy or friend.

Examples of the peculiar satiric vibrancy which occurs when Swift re-enters as enemy, directing his attack to pierce the defenses of the reader himself, are examples of satire of the second person. They are infrequent, for satire is indeed a glass in which men see every image but their own. But examples occur.

The career of Gulliver provides a case in point. It is a matter of common observation that Gulliver develops in depth and seriousness as his story progresses, that his character becomes more profound and his criticism more searching. The sequence of his development is usually thought of as being clear in Books I, II, and IV, and as being, if not strengthened by Book III, yet not disturbed by it. The sequence refers to the narrative as it stands, and not to the books in order of their composition.

Gulliver's progress is usually assumed to be visible in Books I and II alone. Brobdingnag is not only the "large" of a vein of satire already developed in "small," but something new as well. One reason for this view of the two books is the fact that political allegory, which in the first book is characterized by particularity of reference, does not have a commensurate development in Book II. Another reason is that while in Lilliput Gulliver was the victim of ingratitude, petty jealousy, and calumny, in Brobdingnag he met with opposition of a more formidable kind.

His conversations with the King of Brobdingnag are often quoted as examples of Swift's satiric force. In the first encounter with the

King that Gulliver reports he hears "how contemptible a Thing was human Grandeur, which could be mimicked by such diminutive Insects. . . ." Furthermore, to repeat Wotton's phrase, he "sits down under it": "as I was not in a Condition to resent Injuries, so, upon mature Thoughts, I began to doubt whether I were injured or no." [2] A later encounter ends in the King's famous diatribe against "the most pernicious Race of little odious Vermin that Nature ever suffered to crawl upon the Surface of the Earth." [3]

This element of the voyage to Brobdingnag is different in essential quality from anything in Book I. It is an item in the series of events and attitudes which indicates Gulliver's development, or, to adopt another mode of interpretation, which marks his decline into Timonism. Its effect upon the reader, although difficult to define, is powerful. And in some way it involves the complex interrelationships between Swift, Gulliver, and the reader.

It is unnecessary, if not unwise, to decide that in passages of this kind Swift suddenly thrusts himself forward in his own person and makes direct accusations. F. R. Leavis[4] and Robert C. Elliott[5] have suggested that something of this sort takes place, especially in parts of *A Tale of a Tub* which we must examine later. This explanation implies that the art of Gulliver's narrative can be arbitrarily suspended to make way for lectures. But the fiction is not suspended. In whatever degree the reader finds himself accused in these passages, he is self-accused. It is by virtue of the fiction that he is accused at all.

Assurance of another's error fosters a state of mind which is stable, confident, secure. Ridicule of persons not so good as ourselves is reassuring. Much of Swift's satire has this effect. His caustic scorn encourages complacency that we are not as one of these. But there are passages of another sort. These passages have a contrary effect. They bring the mind to precarious equilibrium. They prompt a state of being which is unstable, insecure, and afraid.

The fourth book of the *Travels* is in many ways the fiercest of Swift's satires. Gulliver slowly realizes that he must acknowledge his kinship with the Yahoos. The ritual farewell to the Houyhnhnm master is a relinquishment of his hope to achieve rationality. The book is usually glossed by a citation of Swift's plaintive letter to Pope, despite the fact that Gulliver apparently, and the Yahoos certainly, are somewhat less than *rationis capax.*

[2] [Bk. II, ch. 3.]
[3] [Bk. II, ch. 6.]
[4] "The Irony of Swift," *Determinations* (London: Chatto and Windus, 1934), pp. 94–101.
[5] "Swift's *Tale of a Tub:* An Essay in Problems of Structure," *PMLA,* LXVI (1951), pp. 441–55.

The fourth book is part of the carefully devised fable. It has qualities different from those of a letter to Pope. It has content which cannot be reduced to a simple statement of doctrine. The farewell to the Houyhnhnms is not unrelievedly sententious. Gulliver's parade of sentimentality for the rational is not without its element of incongruity.

The crux of the matter is in the conclusion of the volume, and in the interpretation which one makes of Gulliver's felicity with his English horses. If the perfections of the Houyhnhnms are indeed perfect, and if the people of England are indeed Yahoos, then Swift's final counsel is a counsel of despair. But if the final chapter is read as betraying the doctrine of the Houyhnhnms, the effect is somewhat different.

It should be remembered that upon his return from the Houyhnhnms Gulliver could not endure the presence of other human beings. Their odor offended him. The idea of their caresses nauseated him. Above all he despised in them their sin of pride. Sitting with his commonplace English horses, loathing all human creatures, he said: "I here intreat those who have any Tincture of this absurd Vice, that they will not presume to appear in my Sight." [6]

At this point it seems reasonable to object to Gulliver himself. Although he inveighs against pride, he displays in his own person the external symptoms by which pride may be recognized. The effect is satiric betrayal.

How this procedure may result in satire of the second person is a relatively simple problem, and answerable in simple terms. One of the ancient principles of debate is to induce an opponent to adopt a position which he will later be forced to abandon. In disputation, the moment of victory is the moment at which an adversary is compelled to adjust his premises to the demands of the argument. Aristotle's *Topica* is a description of strategies by which this end may be systematically accomplished. Certain passages of Swift's satire are examples of strategies by which a similar effect can be poetically accomplished.

In Book IV of *Gulliver's Travels* Swift advances a doctrine and wins its acceptance. The doctrine is that of the Houyhnhnms. He then betrays it by his description of Gulliver's final excesses. The reader, convinced on both counts, revises his opinion and is compelled to be aware of the revision. His awareness is satiric effect. The image in the satiric mirror is his own.

Thus interpreted, the final chapter of *Gulliver's Travels* is an example of satire of the second person. . . .

Fundamentally, the items in a rhetorical situation are only two in

[6] [Bk. IV, ch. 12.]

number: author and reader, or orator and audience. The rhetoric of the pulpit in particular strives to bring home to its hearers an immediate and individual sense of dependency, inadequacy, or sin. Some of the most memorable parts of Swift's satires resemble sermon rhetoric in this respect. In fact, it may be primarily this special intimacy which distinguishes Swift's satire from the Mediterranean satire of, for example, Byron, or of Douglas's *South Wind*.

The judgment of history has attributed to Swift greater magnitude, more profundity and seriousness, than to other satirists. Many reasons may be advanced to explain the preference given him, for his genius appears in many aspects. And yet it is possible that in satire, as in tragedy, there is a quality to control the emotions of men which is beyond all other qualities to be desired. This is the quality which Swift displays when his reader, unable to bandy his satire away, sits down quietly under it.

The Satirist Satirized

by Robert C. Elliott

For a number of reasons Swift's *Gulliver* is more difficult to come
to terms with than *Timon* or *The Misanthrope,* even from the limited
point of view which defines our special interest in the works. The
most immediate problem is that of genre. *Timon* and *The Misanthrope*
are plays; no matter how much satire and how many satirists may be
involved, the plays conform to well-established dramatic conventions.
We know the conventions, know in general what to expect in the way
of structure, characterization, etc. But what of *Gulliver's Travels?* It is
a fiction; it is written in prose; it is an "imaginary voyage." So much
one can say, but to say this is to say very little. The imaginary voyage
has taken such an astonishing variety of forms that it seems impossible
to define it as a genre, to say nothing of systematizing its conventions.[1]
Is *Gulliver* a novel? Probably not, although it is not easy to say (except
by arbitrary stipulation) why it is not. Clearly it is satire; but that
is not to say that it is *a* satire. Arthur E. Case, for example, thinks
that it is not: ". . . it would be more accurate and more illuminating
to call it a politico-sociological treatise much of which is couched in
the medium of satire." [2] We shy from using the category "a satire"
today, at least when we are trying to speak precisely, because the term
has lost for us any sense of formal specification.

Why worry about genre? one might ask. Every work is entitled to
its own *donnée.* Why not consider *Gulliver* in its own terms, *sui
generis,* working out from the text its own presuppositions, its own
assumptions? Theoretically the method is feasible, practically very
difficult. As the history of Swift criticism shows, the temptation has
been overpowering to slip from considering the *Travels* as a thing in
itself, to considering it as a kind of confession (Swift's confession), as

"The Satirist Satirized" by Robert C. Elliott. From The Power of Satire *(Princeton:
Princeton University Press, 1960), pp. 184–214. Copyright © 1960 by Princeton
University Press. Reprinted by permission of the publisher.*

[1] See Part One of Philip B. Gove, *The Imaginary Voyage in Prose Fiction* (New
York, 1941).

[2] *Four Essays on Gulliver's Travels* (Princeton, N.J., 1945), p. 105.

a children's tale, as a novel, as a curse, as comedy, as tragedy, as evidence of Swift's lunacy, his coprophilia, whatnot. Some of these uses are doubtless legitimate enough for special purposes; but if we are interested in critical evaluation of *Gulliver's Travels* as a literary work, then we must judge it by the laws of its own conventions, not by the laws of a country to which it owes no allegiance. For this reason we must try to "place" *Gulliver* as best we can.

Lucian tells an amusing parable of how Dionysus, Pan, Silenus, the satyrs, and the maenads invaded India. The Hindus with their massive armies, their elephants, their towers on top of the elephants, thought the invasion absurd. Scouts brought word that the enemy army consisted largely of young clodhoppers with tails and horns, given to dancing about naked, and crazy women who rushed around shouting "Evoe!" The two principal lieutenants were an old man with a gross belly and big ears, and an odd creature built below like a goat. It was impossible not to laugh at them. But when the Indians were finally forced to do battle with the invaders and encountered the whirling, shrieking frenzy of Dionysus' troops, their ponderous array of elephants broke and fled in terror. Lucian makes his point: ". . . most people are in the same state of mind as the Hindoos when they encounter literary novelties, like mine for example. Thinking that what they hear from me will smack of Satyrs and of jokes, in short, of comedy . . . some of them do not come at all, believing it unseemly to come off their elephants and give their attention to the revels of women and the skipping of Satyrs, while others apparently come for something of that kind, and when they find steel instead of ivy, are even then slow to applaud, confused by the unexpectedness of the thing." [3]

In his recent *Anatomy of Criticism* Northrop Frye deals brilliantly with the "steel instead of ivy" puzzle, insofar as it concerns works like *Gulliver's Travels, Candide, Erewhon, Brave New World*—all prose fictions but all dubiously attached to the rubric of the novel.[4] These works Frye calls Menippean satires. The term requires explanation. Menippus was a pugnacious Greek Cynic (third century B.C.) who wrote satires in a mixture of prose and verse. His works have been lost, and most of what we know of him comes from his admirer and professed imitator, Lucian. Menippus figures as a character in several of Lucian's satires, in, for example, the *Icaromennipus* which almost unquestionably influenced Swift. Another imitator of Menippus was Marcus Terentius Varro, the most learned of all the Romans, whose *Saturae Menippeae* were extremely influential but survive today only

[3] "Dionysus," in *Lucian*, trans. Harmon, I, 49–55.
[4] (Princeton, N.J., 1957), pp. 305 ff.

in fragments. The Menippean (or Varronian, as it is sometimes called) tradition was continued by Seneca (*Apocolocyntosis: The Pumpkinification of Claudius*), Petronius (*Satyricon*), and Apuleius (*The Golden Ass*).[5] Quintilian describes the Menippean as an older kind of satire than that written by Lucilius and characterizes it by its mixture of prose and verse.[6] Since his time little has been done to give the form (if it is a form) more precise lineaments. Dryden, for example, uses the term in much the same way as Quintilian used it.

Frye is more ambitious. He attempts to work out the characteristics of a form strict enough to incorporate its own conventions, but flexible enough to include the works mentioned above together with other great mavericks: *The Praise of Folly, Gargantua and Pantagruel, The Anatomy of Melancholy,* the Alice books, etc. He describes the form thus (the prose-verse mixture has, somewhat awkwardly, been dropped as a *differentia*):

> The Menippean satire deals less with people as such than with mental attitudes. Pedants, bigots, cranks, parvenus, virtuosi, enthusiasts, rapacious and incompetent professional men of all kinds, are handled in terms of their occupational approach to life as distinct from their social behavior. The Menippean satire thus resembles the confession in its ability to handle abstract ideas and theories, and differs from the novel in its characterization, which is stylized rather than naturalistic, and presents people as mouthpieces of the ideas they represent. Here again no sharp boundary lines can or should be drawn, but if we compare a character in Jane Austen with a similar character in Peacock we can immediately feel the differences between the two forms. Squire Western belongs to the novel, but Thwackum and Square have Menippean blood in them. . . .
>
> Petronius, Apuleius, Rabelais, Swift, and Voltaire all use a loose-jointed narrative form . . . [that] relies on the free play of intellectual fancy and the kind of humorous observation that produces caricature. It differs . . . from the picaresque form, which has the novel's interest in the actual structure of society. At its most concentrated the Menippean satire presents us with a vision of the world in terms of a single intellectual pattern. The intellectual structure built up from the story makes for violent dislocations in the customary logic of narrative, though the appearance of carelessness that results reflects only the carelessness of the reader or his tendency to judge by a novel-centered conception of fiction. . . .[7]

We must look at some of the formal relations governing the work.

[5] For various reasons Frye later abandons *Menippean* in favor of the term *anatomy,* as in Burton's *Anatomy of Melancholy.*

[6] *Institutio Oratoria,* x, 95, trans. Butler, IV, 55.

[7] *Anatomy of Criticism,* pp. 309–10.

Swift gives us little "outside" information about how or when Gulliver
wrote the account of his travels. Richard Sympson, the fictive publisher,
said to be a relative of Gulliver on his mother's side, writes that he
corrected the Captain's papers; and Gulliver himself complains that
his manuscript has been tampered with. That is all we know. Within
the work itself, however, is evidence that Gulliver composed his
memoirs as an elderly man, after he had retired from his unfortunate
life on the sea. Several times in the narrative Gulliver looks back in
chronological time to previous voyages, bringing his experience from
them to bear on a "present" predicament; but he never looks forward
specifically to "future" adventures as commentary on what is happening at the moment. Still, it is apparent from casual comments in the
early voyages that a whole realm of "future" experience is available
to the writer. For example, at the end of Part ı Gulliver describes his
preparations for shipping out again: "My Daughter *Betty* (who is
now well married, and has Children) was then at her Needle-Work"
(p. 64).[8] Between "now"—at the time of writing—and "then" lie the
years of Gulliver's three subsequent voyages, plus five years which
elapse between his final return to England and the composition of
the work.

The Gulliver who writes, then, is Gulliver the misanthrope who
stuffs his nose with tobacco leaves and keeps a long table between
himself and his wife. It is he who "creates" the ship's surgeon—a
man capable of longing for the tongue of Demosthenes so that he may
celebrate his country in a style equal to its unparalleled merits. Given
the emotional and intellectual imbalance of the old seaman, he is
remarkably successful in producing an objective portrait of himself as
he was in time long past.

The actual, as opposed to the fictive, situation, of course, is that
Swift has created two dominant points of view to control the materials
of the *Travels*: that of his favorite *ingénu* (the younger Gulliver) and
that of the misanthrope. The technique has obvious advantages. An
ingénu is a superb agent of indirect satire as he roams the world
uncritically recording or even embracing the folly which it is the
satirist's business to undermine: "*Flimnap*, the Treasurer, is allowed
to cut a Caper on the strait Rope, at least an Inch higher than any other
Lord in the whole Empire" (p. 22).[9] On the other hand, a misanthrope
can develop all the great power of direct, hyperbolic criticism. By al-
lowing Gulliver, an uncritical lover of man, to become an uncritical
hater of man, Swift has it both ways.

The technique is not that of the novelist, however. Swift pays little
regard to psychological consistency; Gulliver's character can hardly be

[8] [Bk. I, ch. 8. All page references are to the Davis-Williams edition, 1941.]
[9] [Bk. I, ch. 3.]

said to develop; it simply changes. If one takes seriously the premise that Gulliver writes his memoirs after his rebirth, then many passages in the early voyages turn out to be inconsistent and out of character. "There are," says Gulliver of Lilliput, "some Laws and Customs in this Empire very peculiar; and if they were not so directly contrary to those of my own dear Country, I should be tempted to say a little in their Justification" (p. 42).[10] (The laws from Swift's point of view, from the point of view of reason, are excellent.) Here Gulliver is trapped in a conflict between his patriotism and his reason; as he is an *ingénu* his patriotism wins. But note the tense: "I should be tempted"; that is, now—at the time of writing. Given this tense, and given the logic of the controlling situation, it must follow that this is the utterance of Gulliver as he composes the work. At the time he writes, however, Gulliver is committed so irrevocably to the claims of reason that the appeal of patriotism could not possibly have meaning for him—could not, that is, if we assume general consistency in Gulliver's character.

Similar examples of what in novels would be called inconsistency in characterization can be found in nearly all Menippean satires. . . .[11]

Similar as the management of perspective is in the passages from the *Satyricon* and from *Gulliver,* and successful as they both are in achieving the illusion of objective reality, there is still a great difference in their respective tones. The difference is wholly a matter of style. Petronius manages brilliantly to capture the accent and intonation of the speaker himself. The rhythm of the speech, the syntax, the vocabulary—all bespeak the amiable vulgarian who is part of what he describes. Unquestionably here the style is the man. Not so with Swift. His concerns when dealing with human beings are characteristically more abstract. Oddly, the conversation with the courtier is one of the few in the *Travels* presented as direct quotation; conversations are normally reported in Gulliver's hurried, summarizing way as indirect discourse: I informed him that. . . . I dwelt long upon. . . . I computed. . . . He asked what. . . . He then desired to know. . . . It is as though Swift deliberately avoided the direct confrontation in which individuals would speak with their own voices. But the passage under consideration is in direct discourse: "You are to know, said he, that several Committees of Council have been lately called in the most private Manner on your Account. . . ."; the monologue continues for several pages. Still, we have no real sense that what is said represents a *personal* voice at all. One reason is that the bulk of what the friend reports is something between summary and quotation of what other people have said:

---

[10] [Bk. I, ch. 6.]
[11] [A discussion of Petronius' *Satyricon* is omitted.]

> *Bolgolam,* the Admiral, could not preserve his Temper; but rising up
> in Fury, said, he wondered how the Secretary durst presume to give
> his Opinion for preserving the Life of a Traytor: That the Services
> you had performed, were, by all true Reasons of State, the great Aggrava-
> tion of your Crimes; that you, who were able to extinguish the Fire,
> by discharge of Urine in her Majesty's Apartment (which he mentioned
> with Horror) might, at another time, raise an Inundation by the same
> Means, to drown the whole Palace. . . . (p. 54)[12]

These are the rhythms that Gulliver as author habitually employs
in recording conversation. The speaker is allowed almost no individual
tone, as a consequence of which our sense of him as a person is vague.
Yet we know unmistakably his relation to certain ideas and moral
attitudes. Through him we are shown the motivation of admirals,
the "magnanimity" of princes, the objectivity of friends in discussing
one's own demise. Insubstantial as he may be, he is an excellent con-
ductor of satire.

But if the characters Gulliver meets on his travels lack individuality,
if their voices lack the kind of realism we find in the voice of Encolpius'
nameless companion, how different the texture of most of the rest of
the work! Swift claims in a letter to Pope that a Bishop in Dublin
had read the *Travels* and decided it was full of improbable lies—he
hardly believed a word of it; it is as good testimony as any to the
extraordinary illusion of verisimilitude Swift imparts to the narrative.[13]
"There is an Air of Truth apparent through the whole," says Richard
Sympson, the "publisher," attributing it to the circumstantiality of the
"plain and simple" style, to which he condescends a little, and of which
Gulliver is proud.[14] Gulliver can hardly be conceived of apart from
his style; he defines himself by the way he writes, particularly at the
beginning:

> My Father had a small Estate in *Nottinghamshire;* I was the Third
> of five Sons. He sent me to *Emanuel-College* in *Cambridge,* at Fourteen
> Years old, where I resided three Years, and applied my self close to my
> Studies. . . . I was bound Apprentice to Mr. *James Bates,* an eminent
> Surgeon in *London,* with whom I continued four Years. . . . I took
> Part of a small House in the *Old Jury;* and being advised to alter my
> Condition, I married Mrs. *Mary Burton,* second Daughter to Mr. *Edmond
> Burton,* Hosier, in *Newgatestreet,* with whom I received four Hundred
> Pounds for a Portion. (pp. 3–4)[15]

To define one's life, one enumerates the solid, unproblematic facts

[12] [Bk. I, ch. 7.]
[13] *Correspondence,* ed. Ball, III, 368.
[14] [The Publisher to the Reader.]
[15] [Bk. I, ch. 1.]

that have gone to make it, and one uses solid, unproblematic sentences—simple and straightforward as one's own character.

As the account proceeds the factual texture is thickened:

> By an Observation, we found ourselves in the Latitude of 30 degrees
> 2 Minutes South. Twelve of our Crew were dead by immoderate Labour,
> and ill Food; the rest were in a very weak Condition. On the fifth of
> *November,* which was the beginning of Summer in those Parts, the
> Weather being very hazy, the Seamen spyed a Rock, within half a Cable's
> length of the Ship; but the Wind was so strong, that we were driven
> directly upon it, and immediately split. Six of the crew, of whom I was
> one, having let down the Boat into the Sea, made a Shift to get clear of
> the Ship, and the Rock. . . . In about half an Hour the Boat was
> overset by a sudden Flurry from the North. What became of my Companions in the Boat, as well as of those who escaped on the Rock, or
> were left in the Vessel, I cannot tell; but conclude they were all lost.
> For my own Part, I swam as Fortune directed me. . . . (pp. 4–5)[16]

The lack of modulation is striking. The predominately declarative sentences set out the things that happen in their concrete particularity, piling them up but making no differentiation among them. There is something monstrous in the way that Gulliver can describe the taking of a geographical fix, the deaths of twelve seamen, the wreck of the ship, the loss of his companions, his inability to sit up after his sleep ashore—all in sentences similar in structure and identical in tone. Ordinarily, by his style a writer judges his material, places it for his reader in the context of moral experience. Here, the lack of modulation in the style is a moral commentary on the writer—on Gulliver. Even the King of Brobdingnag is struck by this aspect of Gulliver's style: "He was amazed how so impotent and groveling an Insect as I (these were his Expressions) could entertain such inhuman Ideas, and in so familiar a Manner as to appear wholly unmoved at all the Scenes of Blood and Desolation, which I had painted. . . ." (pp. 118–19)[17]

But while we may equate the impassivity of tone with an impassivity of sensibility, we are overwhelmed by the impression of Gulliver's commitment to hard, undeniable fact. Dr. Johnson speaks finely of Swift's "vigilance of minute attention"; we see it most impressively as Gulliver records his reaction to the Lilliputians. The pages are peppered with citations of numbers, figures, dimensions: I count over thirty such citations in the last three paragraphs of Chapter One, each figure increasing our sense of the reality of the scene; for nothing, we tend to think, is so real as number. Gulliver's style approximates an

[16] [Bk. I, ch. 1.]
[17] [Bk. II, ch. 7.]

ideal of seventeenth-century scientists: "the marriage of words and things," the deliverance, as Thomas Sprat puts it in a famous passage, of "so many *things*, almost in an equal number of words." [18] Swift (not Gulliver, now) is parodying the life-style that finds its only meaning in things, that lives entirely in the particularity of externals, without being able to discriminate among them. This explains in part the function of the scatological passages of Parts i and ii which have been found so offensive. The style also helps prepare for the satire on language theory in Part iii. But, parody or no, Gulliver's style is a marvellous instrument for narration, building easily and with increasing fluidity the substantiality of his world.

Gulliver, then, succeeds in the novelist's great task of creating the illusion of reality. But again we must recall that he is not a novelist. The reality he creates is one of externals only. He does not create a sense of reality about himself—or rather, to step now outside the framework of the *Travels*, Swift does not create a sense of reality about Gulliver. Gulliver is not a character in the sense that Tom Jones, say, is a character. He has the most minimal subjective life; even his passion at the end is hardly rooted in personality. He is, in fact, an abstraction, manipulated in the service of satire. To say this of the principal character of a novel would be damning; but to say it of a work written according to the conventions of Lucian's *A True Story*, the *Satyricon, Gargantua* is simply to describe.

The paucity of Gulliver's inner life needs little documentation. To be sure, he is shown as decent and kindly and honorable at the beginning: we are delighted with his stalwart vindication of the honor of the Treasurer's wife, whom malicious gossip accused of having an affair with him. But his life is primarily of the senses. He sees—how superbly he sees!—he hears, smells, feels. Poke him and he twitches; but there is little evidence of rational activity. The *leaping* and *creeping* contest at the Lilliputian court is a diversion for him, nothing more; he sees no resemblance between it and practices in any other court in the world. Except for an occasional (dramatically inconsistent) episode where he is startled into an expression of bitterness, Gulliver's is a life without nuance. The nuances are there, of course, everywhere, but must be supplied by the reader.

In the second voyage Gulliver is even more obviously a mouthpiece for ideas (usually absurd or despicable ideas set up to be subverted by the satire) than a character in his own right. True, he is occasionally reflective: "Undoubtedly Philosophers are in the Right," he muses, as he cowers in fear of being squashed under the foot of the Brobdingnagian, "when they tell us, that nothing is great or little otherwise

[18] *History of the Royal Society* (London, 1667), p. 113.

than by Comparison" (p. 71).[19] And his own thoughts may even reflect satiric insight. On one occasion the King of Brobdingnag remarks on how human (i.e., Brobdingnagian) grandeur can be mimicked by insects like Gulliver. Gulliver is furious; but the King's mockery works insidiously, and Gulliver begins to wonder whether he has been injured or not:

> . . . if I had then beheld a Company of *English* Lords and Ladies in their Finery and Birth-day Cloaths, acting their several Parts in the most courtly Manner of Strutting, and Bowing and Prating; to say the Truth, I should have been strongly tempted to laugh as much at them as this King and his Grandees did at me. (p. 91; cf. p. 108) [20]

Most of the time, however, Gulliver either is impenetrably innocent or embraces the pride and the folly of European civilization with insatiable zeal—all in the interest of the most mordant satire. . . .[21]

Still, the drift of Gulliver's attitude is clearly toward the misanthropic; and when in the last voyage he finds himself caught between the fixed positions of the Yahoos and the Houyhnhnms, he is quick to make his unnaturally extreme choice. There is logic to his change. Like Tennyson's Ulysses, he is part of all that he has known: he has heard the King of Brobdingnag, he has learned the dirty secrets of modern history at Glubbdubdrib, he has suffered at the hands of the most abandoned criminals—those who composed his crew. In a way his misanthropy has been earned. But this is really beside the point; for Gulliver's change comes about, not in any psychologically plausible way, but because the final, desperate, internal demands of the satire force him to change.

Part IV of the *Travels* is schematically so like Part II that comparison is inevitable. The intellectual climaxes of the voyages come in conversations between Gulliver and his host of the moment: The King in Brobdingnag, the grey steed in Houyhnhnm-land. In Part II, as we have seen, Swift prepared the scene carefully, giving it a dramatic setting and structure like that of the formal verse satire. The conversations in Part IV are less sharply dramatized, the climactic chapters five and six hardly being set apart from other talks in which Gulliver has explained to his Master who and what he is. Gulliver discourses on war, law, commerce, medicine, ministers-of-state, the nobility—the subjects of his rhapsody in Part II—but this time in a flood of vituperation rarely matched in literature. The Houyhnhnm has little role in this onslaught except to ask an occasional question. He is as shadowy an interlocutor as some of Juvenal's. The whole tremendous force

[19] [Bk. II, ch. 1.]
[20] [Bk. II, ch. 3; cf. Bk. II, ch. 5.]
[21] [The discussion of the remainder of Bk. II and Bk. III is omitted.]

of these dozen pages is carried by Gulliver's diatribe. For comparison one thinks of Shakespeare's Timon; yet the difference in tone between the two modes of utterance is enormous. Timon vents personal rage; his hatred comes boiling forth in a mighty, prolonged curse. Gulliver here expresses no hatred; he professes simply to be laying before his Master "the whole State of Europe," as he says. His vein is cold, analytic, impersonal. . . .

The two chapters of unimpassioned tirade (one can speak of this style only in terms of paradox) slide imperceptibly between indirect and direct discourse, between the imperfect and the historical present tense, producing sometimes a feeling of dramatic immediacy, sometimes a feeling of rapid survey. As one "fact" is coldly and neatly balanced upon another, there is little modulation in tone, no attempt at climax, no dramatic shift into direct discourse as in Part II; it is as though Swift, here at the apogee of Gulliver's progress, scorned such rhetorical tricks, as Gulliver himself claims to do, content to let his "plain Matter of Fact" carry the burden. In its impassive efficiency the style reminds one in some respects of an official Air Force report of a successful bombing raid on a large city.

But this is overstated. The most obvious rhetorical device used here is the exaggeration which pushes Gulliver's account into the realm of the grotesque. We can no more believe in the reality of Gulliver's lawyers than we can believe in Falstaff's tales of his prowess at Gadshill: the two passages have something in common. These lawyers are superhuman, true giants of duplicity. They belong in a far more ideal world than any we know; we can even (unless we are too shocked, or unless we are lawyers) laugh. For obscure reasons, the exaggeration makes our pleasure possible, while it in no way weakens the destructive force of the satiric attack.

Swift uses another favorite stylistic maneuver here—the incongruous catalogue:

> . . . vast Numbers of our People are compelled to seek their Livelihood by Begging, Robbing, Stealing, Cheating, Pimping, Forswearing, Flattering, Suborning, Forging, Gaming, Lying, Fawning, Hectoring, Voting, Scribling, Stargazing, Poysoning, Whoring, Canting, Libelling, Free-thinking, and the like Occupations: Every one of which Terms, I was at much Pains to make him understand (p. 236).[22]

It is a noxious enumeration, saved from mere ranting by the incongruity. Syntactical equivalence in a list of this kind obviously implies moral equivalence. Thus star-gazing and canting come to equal murder. At first sight the conjunction is amusing (as is the picture of Gulliver spending days in the intricate job of translation); but the final sa-

[22] [Bk. IV, ch. 6.]

tiric insinuation is that in a sense the equivalence holds; common to all the "Occupations" is a perversion of reason and morality which can lead only to disaster. Precisely this is the burden of the great satire contemporary with *Gulliver's Travels*, Pope's *Dunciad*.

Such rhetorical flourishes are rare in the climactic two chapters of the fourth voyage, however. Their over-riding function is to develop with cold implacability the horror of English civilization as Gulliver sees it. Like Timon and like Alceste, Gulliver has assumed the role of satirist, and from this point on he broadens his target to include humanity itself: "When I thought of my Family, my Friends, my Countrymen, or human Race in general, I considered them as they really were, *Yahoos* in Shape and Disposition" (p. 262).[23]

Against the destructiveness of Gulliver's onslaught, we look for the kind of positives that are evident in the episode of the Brobding-nagian King. We naturally turn to the Houyhnhnms who represent to Gulliver (and surely in some sense to Swift) one pole of an antin-omy: "The Perfection of Nature" over against the repulsiveness of Yahoo-man. Both Gulliver and the Houyhnhnms are at pains to point out wherein Houyhnhnm perfection lies. It is first physical: Gulliver is lost in awe of the "Strength, Comeliness and Speed" of the horses, whereas he can view his own person only with detestation. The Hou-yhnhnms themselves are emphatic on the deficiencies of the human physique: Gulliver's hands are too soft to walk on, his nails too short to claw with, his face flat, nose prominent, eyes misplaced, etc. (pp. 226–27).[24] Houyhnhnm perfection is next mental: the horses' lives are "wholly governed" by reason, an infallible faculty, at least to the degree that there is nothing "problematical" about it; reason strikes them with immediate conviction, so that opinion and controversy are unknown. Their perfection is finally moral. They lead austere lives devoted to temperance, industry, and cleanliness; they have no idea of what is evil in a rational creature, have no vice, no lusts, and their passions are firmly controlled by the rational faculty. Their principal virtues are friendship and benevolence, which extend to the whole race; and love as we understand it is unknown. For Gulliver the Houyhnhnms are the repository of all that is good.

Here are positives in abundance, the only question being whether they are unqualifiedly Swift's positives. Most critics have felt that they are and that *Gulliver's Travels* (to say nothing of Swift's character) suffers thereby. . . .

[23] [Bk. IV, ch. 10.] Gulliver is even capable of a macabre wit: "And, to set forth the Valour of my own dear Countrymen, I assured him, that I had seen them blow up a Hundred Enemies at once in a Siege . . . and beheld the dead Bodies drop down in Pieces from the Clouds, to the great Diversion of all the Spectators" (p. 231)—[Bk. IV, ch. 5].

[24] [Bk. IV, ch. 4.]

It seems likely that a close reading of Gulliver's fourth voyage is such a shocking experience as to anesthetize the feeling for the ludicrous of even the most sensitive readers (perhaps *particularly* the most sensitive readers). I do not mean to deny the horror of the work, which is radical; but the horror is ringed, as it were, by Swift's mocking laughter. For example, Coleridge is outraged at the way "the horse discourses on the human frame with the grossest prejudices that could possibly be inspired by vanity and self-opinion." Human limbs, Coleridge stoutly insists, are much better suited for climbing and for managing tools than are fetlocks. Swift lacks "reverence for the original frame of man." [25] True, Swift did lack reverence for human clay; but he also wrote the scene of the Houyhnhnm's denigration of the human body as comedy. It is very funny. It is a kind of parody of the eighteenth century's concern over man's coveting various attributes of the animals, "the strength of bulls, the fur of bears." It is even connected, as we shall see, with the theme of man's coveting supra-human reason. It has the same satirical function as the parallel passage in the second voyage, where the Brobdingnagian philosophers determine after close examination of his form that Gulliver is incapable of preserving his life "either by Swiftness, or climbing of Trees, or digging Holes in the Earth" and must be a *Lusus Naturae*—this kind of determination being "to the unspeakable Advancement of human Knowledge" (pp. 87–88).[26] The equine chauvinism of the Houyhnhnms, amusing as it is, undercuts their authority; it must raise doubts in our minds about their adequacy as guides to *human* excellence, to say nothing of the adequacy of Gulliver, who wants to become a horse and whose capacities in matters requiring moral and intellectual discrimination have not been such as to inspire confidence. . . .

The violence of Gulliver's alienation, his demand (like that of Timon and Alceste) for the absolute, incapacitate him for what Lionel Trilling calls the "common routine" of life—that feeling for the ordinary, the elemental, the enduring which validates all tragic art.[27] Each of Gulliver's voyages begins with a departure from the common routine, each ends with a return to it—to his wife "Mrs. *Mary Burton,* second Daughter to Mr. *Edmond Burton,* Hosier" [28] and their children. This commonplace family represents a fixed point of stability and calm in Gulliver's life, a kind of norm of humble though enduring human values. Gulliver comes from this life, his early literary style is an

[25] [*Coleridge's Miscellaneous Criticism,* ed. I. M. Raysor, 1936, p. 130.]

[26] [Bk. II, ch. 3.]

[27] Lionel Trilling, "Wordsworth and the Iron Time," *Kenyon Review,* XII (1950), p. 495, reprinted as "Wordsworth and the Rabbis," in *The Opposing Self* (New York, 1955).

[28] [Bk. I, ch. 1.]

emblem of it; and it is against the background given by the common routine that his wild rejection shows so startlingly. His first sight of his family after the years of absence produced in him only "Hatred, Disgust and Contempt. . . . As soon as I entered the House, my Wife took me in her Arms, and kissed me; at which not having been used to the Touch of that odious Animal for so many Years, I fell in a Swoon for almost an Hour" (p. 273).[29]

In short, Gulliver's *idée fixe* is tested in the world of human experience. The notion that all men are Yahoos cannot accommodate a Don Pedro de Mendez any more than it can accommodate the long-suffering family at Redriff. But this is our own ironic insight, unavailable to Gulliver, who has never been capable of evaluating the significance of his own experience. Gulliver persistently moulds the world according to his idea of it, instead of moulding his idea according to the reality of things—which must include the Portuguese. Such behavior defines comic absurdity as Bergson expounds it. In other contexts this kind of "inversion of common sense" is characteristic of insanity.[30]

[29] [Bk. IV, ch. 11.]
[30] Henri Bergson, *Laughter*, trans. Cloudesley Brereton and Fred Rothwell (London, 1911), pp. 183–85.

The Satiric Victim

by E. W. Rosenheim

The perennially challenging pages of *Gulliver's Travels* receive, I believe, considerable illumination from a distinction between the satiric and non-satiric. Many of the studies which have dwelt upon the "background" of this most famous of Swift's works have, whether deliberately or not, expanded the satiric dimension of the book. The result of many researches has been to supply precisely the historic particulars which are under attack by Swift, to transform, in increasing amounts, parts of the fantasy which the work appears to be at its most superficial level into hostile comment upon specific phenomena in Swift's world.

Such discoveries tend to reinforce the most familiar of all clichés about *Gulliver's Travels*—the proposition that an apparently charming story, while undeniably appealing as such to the youthful or unsophisticated reader, is actually a bitter satiric attack upon authentic follies and abuses. This generalization implies that a "proper" reading of the text, a reading conducted in complete awareness of its most important qualities, must proceed on the assumption that *Gulliver's Travels* is, in its totality, a satiric construction and that the attractive fiction which supports the entire work is merely the mask or vehicle for a sustained satiric assault.

There are, however, great difficulties inherent in such a view. The initial problem—that the objects of Swift's satire are a widely diffuse assortment, sporadically and fragmentarily treated—is not insuperable; *A Tale of a Tub* presents similar obstacles to any search for "satiric unity," yet it is an essentially satiric work, sufficiently well organized to be intelligible and effective as such. A far more serious impediment to the consideration of *Gulliver's Travels* as primarily satiric is the magnitude, both in terms of sheer quantity within the text and of our response to the total work, of elements which do not conform to the concept of satire we have been employing. Unless, as seems unlikely, the discovery of specific targets proceeds in the future with vastly

"The Satiric Victim" by E. W. Rosenheim. From Swift and the Satirist's Art *(Chicago: University of Chicago Press, 1963), pp. 90–97. Copyright © 1963 by the University of Chicago Press. Reprinted by permission of the publisher.*

multiplied results, many pages of *Gulliver's Travels* will continue to appeal to us for reasons which have little to do with satiric significance.

Within recent years, indeed, there has been some tendency for scholars to ignore the satiric character of *Gulliver's Travels* and, in particular, to impose upon it some of the modes of analysis traditionally applied to purely comic literature. Approaches of this kind are laudable to the extent that they are invited by genuine comic qualities in the book, but one notes in such studies a failure, analogous to that found in purely "satiric" descriptions, to take into account those elements which have no demonstrable relevance to the attainment of comic ends. Thus to regard the work as exclusively either a "satire" or a "comedy" produces interpretations which are inevitably fragmentary. The *Travels* provides, moreover, an excellent illustration of the inadequacy of such hybrid species as "comic satire" or "satiric comedy," if only because it contains so many elements which are grimly non-comic and so many others to which it seems impossible to apply the word "satire" in any productive sense. Above all, to thrust *Gulliver's Travels* into the monolithic mold of a single literary species is an act of violence precisely because the ever surprising *different* literary experiences it provides constitute one of its chief claims upon our enthusiastic attention.

It is, I think, possible to discuss *Gulliver's Travels* adequately only if we are prepared to distinguish between the effects of comedy and of satire, to recognize that these different effects may be sought in closely related passages or even concurrently in a single work, and to suspend our concern for the book's unity in order to discover what Swift is actually doing in every considerable portion of the book.

Thus, for example, I believe we must recognize that the charm and humor of the first book have far greater effect than do any of its satiric procedures—even when we take quite literally all the suggestions which have been made about the correspondence between the Lilliputian world and that of eighteenth-century Europe. The problem of Swift's dominant motive remains insoluble. We cannot reconstruct his intentions and decide whether Lilliput was to him, above all, the satiric arena in which the follies and injustices which burned within his memory would be properly exposed, or whether, on the other hand, the resemblances between his minuscule kingdom and the court of England were satiric touches, added to an original conception of droll fantasy. Whatever his actual motives, however, the fiction, with its intrinsic comic appeal, towers above all satiric design. There is abundant historic reference, but it emerges piecemeal. Our amusement is sporadically elicited at the expense of Walpole or George I or Queen Anne or the conduct of British foreign and domestic affairs; we are aware that the book succeeds in exposing the British court, reduced in stature and with its infirmities accordingly magnified, isolated, and held up to ridicule.

But the reduction and exposure of the particular remain the secondary accomplishments of the Voyage to Lilliput. Its stature in the history of literature is essentially the result of pure imaginative creation, the creation of a world of impossible yet credible homunculi, rendered comic by their physical and moral resemblances to mankind *in general.* To the extent that Gulliver himself and the plight into which he is thrust constitute a true satiric device, he must be equated with a historic counterpart, and obviously we may speak of him, at different points, as the spokesman for a disgruntled Swift or the alter ego of a martyred Harley or Bolingbroke. Far more than these, however, his is the role of ordinary, unspecified man, discomfited by a marvelous imaginative situation from which he is able at last happily to extricate himself in keeping with traditional comic formula.

Gulliver's ineptness among the Lilliputians—like his insignificance among the Brobdingnagians—is not a weakness which can be attributed to any identifiable group or person; it is the result of his normal, his universal human qualities, in large part simply of his ordinary human size. The moral frailties he displays—inflexibility and vanity, for example—are generic human weaknesses of precisely the sort we find exploited in comic characterization and action. It is true, of course, that Gulliver is not regularly an object of ridicule, whether comic or satiric, for he appears more frequently in the role of intelligent observer as well as in that of a "hero," whose plight lays claim, to some extent at least, upon our sympathetic indignation. But to the extent—and it is not a very great extent—that Gulliver is a just victim of his own frailties, he is a comic rather than satiric victim, and it is accordingly to the qualities of the Lilliputians themselves that we must look for Swift's satiric target.

It is true that, with the exception of the "Utopian" sixth chapter,[1] the Lilliputians appear rather contemptible than otherwise. Where our contempt is leavened with laughter, where the Lilliputians are authentically comic, it is almost always in a situation arising out of the basic fiction of Book I, in a dilemma or embarrassment attributable to their stature. On occasion, the stature itself is the chief source of their discomfiture; this is true of many of their laughable attempts to deal properly with their giant visitor. At other times, however, their stature is employed to augment the ludicrous effect of their complacency, arrogance, and shortsightedness, all of which are displayed as generic human failings. The great image—whether comic, poetic, or philosophic—whereby man in his pride is reduced to the

---

[1] Where it seems useful, I refer to the text of *Gulliver's Travels* as it appears in Davis's *Prose Works,* XI. The sixth chapter is found at pp. 41–50.

stature and power of one of the lesser animals yet retains his vision of himself as the potent center of the universe is, understandably enough, an inexhaustible source of critical discussion. It is, indeed, the dominant fiction of Book I, if not of the entire *Travels*, both because of its originality and because of the very universality with which it exposes man in his myopic self-esteem.

But the particularized strictures of satire, within the Voyage to Lilliput, proceed in an essentially autonomous fashion. Against the basically comic episodes attending on the capture and custody of Gulliver, against even such an incident as the saving of the royal palace (which, whether or not it is the satiric representation of Queen Anne's distress over *A Tale of a Tub* or the Treaty of Utrecht, is certainly most effective as a magnificent bit of wholly imaginative ribaldry), there proceed the attacks upon specific persons and policies which have little or nothing to do with the central giant-among-pygmies device. The attacks upon Walpole and Nottingham, the exposure by reduction to absurdity of political patronage and preferment and of religious factionalism, the ultimate excoriation of Whig policy during and after the War of the Spanish Succession are carried out on grounds which are very indirectly connected with the Lilliputian's size or its contrast with Gulliver's stature. There are, of course, moments of amusement, when one transiently recalls that the moral depravity and vanity under attack are the qualities of creatures only six inches high. These are, however, mere comic by-products, as in this case they must be, if the satire is to have its full effect. For the intrigue and ingratitude of the Whig ministry must be seen as a real violation of the rules of decent human behavior rather than the imagined transgressions of the tiny inhabitants of a mythical kingdom.

The explication of the First Book of *Gulliver's Travels* as satire, therefore, provides a very partial, although important, account both of its structure and its total effect. In the first five chapters, little is to be gained by establishing specific objects of satiric attack; the fictional situation is compelling and the imaginary dilemma of Gulliver is the central source of amusement. The "intruding" sixth chapter, with its characterization of Lilliputian institutions (so inconsistent with the context provided by the rest of the book that Gulliver must explain and justify it)[2] is largely satiric and, to the extent that it is satiric, quite superfluous within the fictional construction. As the book progresses, it is precisely at those points at which the giant-among-pygmies situation ceases to provide interest and amusement that the search for the particularized objects of genuine satire becomes necessary.

[2] "In relating these and the following Laws, I would only be understood to mean the original Institutions, and not the most scandalous Corruptions into which these People are fallen by the degenerate Nature of Man" (p. 44).

From the tiny kingdom come manifestations of treachery and ingratitude for which we are unprepared; a grotesque bill of impeachment,
largely without Lilliputian stamp, is reproduced in full (pp. 52-53);[3]
Gulliver's position becomes untenable for reasons which have nothing
directly to do with his size but with the special reaction of his hosts
to a special series of occurrences. What, as pure fictional comedy of
the sort with which the book begins, would be humorless and rather
artless acquires meaning and relevance only because Swift's assault—
and our attention—are now directed not to a mythical kingdom but to
the vexed particulars of English history following the Peace of Utrecht.
In effect, the comic fiction which has been developed by the earlier
chapters yields, toward the conclusion of the book, to a series of satiric
incidents in which the attack depends only tenuously upon the central
conceit of the microcosmic kingdom.

I have already said a good deal to suggest that I find this comic
conceit, with its originality, its delightful elaboration, and its mocking assault upon the complacency of mankind in general, to be the
chief source of satisfaction in the voyage to Lilliput. There are, no
doubt, those who would assert that the satire of the later chapters, if
only because of its location, constitutes the point to which the entire book is directed, that the beguiling fiction is merely an initial
device which leads us to the bitter attack on Whig policy which is the
true "climax" of the voyage. Granted it is possible—although by no
means necessary—to assert the primacy either of the satiric or the
comic in the first book, I should argue only that two very different
kinds of thing are achieved within its pages. And I should suggest,
moreover, that the awareness that particular men, institutions, episodes,
and beliefs are under attack is the distinctive mark of our response to
whatever is truly satiric in this engaging fable.

Many of the things we have said about the voyage to Lilliput apply
equally to Gulliver's sojourn among the Brobdingnagians. Both the
comic power and philosophic suggestiveness of his encounter with
these huge creatures are, of course, strongly enhanced by the contrast
between the basic dilemmas, with respect to human size, of the first
two books. As in the voyage to Lilliput, Gulliver's principal difficulties
are the result of his size, coupled, to be sure, with varying manifestations of vanity, ineffectual valor, and timidity. And again, Swift is
willing to exploit whatever aspect of the discrepancy between the size
of Gulliver and his hosts seems convenient for comic purposes. Gulliver
is at times the frustrated, squeaking victim of his vastly powerful captors; in other passages, notably those in which his stature provides him
with "microscopic" vision of the giants, the Brobdingnagians them-

[3] [Bk. I, ch. 7.]

selves are held up to comic exposure. There are, again, transient satiric thrusts, achieved through a variety of techniques which range from parody[4] to the malicious fantasy which attacks the Maids of Honor. With the dialogues between Gulliver and the Brobdingnagian king, however, the comic quality becomes secondary in the presence of the most sustained satire we have yet encountered in the *Travels*. The dialogue, to be sure, remains closely related to the central fictional conceit, unlike the events which conclude the voyage to Lilliput, for Gulliver's tiny stature and comparative impotence lend a particular irony to his grandiose account of western civilization. It is, of course, the ludicrous size of his tiny visitor which, at the most obvious level, prompts the king's famous characterization of Gulliver's countrymen as "little odious vermin." On the other hand, the essence of the satiric procedure, whereby the legal, political, and ecclesiastical institutions of England are exposed in a manner to justify the king's reaction, does not depend upon the contrast in stature between the two parties to the dialogue. Swift's technique here is largely that of heavy sarcasm in which the naïvely boastful Gulliver parades before the king a highly selective account of the English state, while the king responds with the devastating penetration of the *faux ingénu*.

[4] Stylistic parody is relatively rare in the *Travels*, and where it appears is, in one way or another, made compatible with the broad outlines of Gulliver's character. The nautical jargon (p. 68) [Bk. II, ch. 1] with which Swift apes such models as those found in Samuel Sturmy's *Mariner's Magazine* is entirely appropriate for a sailor, while the scientific explanation of the Flying Island is plainly offered as a "Philosophical Account" (pp. 151–54) [Bk. III, ch. 3]. In his almost exclusive reliance upon narrative events, Swift thus severely limits the use which he can make of a satiric device he elsewhere employs with major effects.

Gulliver in Laputa

by Kathleen Williams

The insecurity and uncertainty of direction we feel at the end of the "Voyage to Brobdingnag" is heightened in Book III. The success of this book is not at all easy for a modern reader to gauge. Its sharp contrast in method, with the grotesque figures of the Laputans and the excursions into magic and immortality, certainly breaks the atmosphere of moral realism which pervades the voyages to Lilliput, Brobdingnag, and Houyhnhnm-land; even the rational horses belong to a world of morality, not of fantasy. This third book, the latest written, would be, by us, the least missed. But on the other hand the fantasy world of Laputa, in its madness and delusion, still further shakes our wits and our confidence before the final resolution of Book IV, and the Laputan lunacies have, after all, a moral connotation as we can see if we remember *A Tale of a Tub*. But for us, to whom the scientific outlook is a commonplace, it is not so easy to see the "Voyage to Laputa" in terms of modern vice and traditional virtue, and we find it less striking than the other voyages, where moral problems are more overtly considered though their presentation is influenced by contemporary thinking. Only the episode of the Struld-brugs of Luggnagg, unencumbered as it is by topical satire, strikes us with the immediate force and the moral emphasis of the second and fourth books, for to a modern reader scientific experiment is a less acceptable example of irrelevant thinking than are the speculations of Burnet or of Thomas Vaughan. Swift's opinion of the scientific achievement of his day is, in itself, inadequate, and considered as an attack on science the third book must seem wrongheaded and unfair. But considered as what it really is, an allegorical presentation of the evils of a frivolous attitude to life, it is consistent and effective, however unjust we may consider Swift's chosen allegory to be.

For the visit to Laputa itself, and to the subject land of Balnibarbi, has a more serious intention than the topical one of ridiculing the Royal Society. The flying island, though it has a precise relationship

"Gulliver in Laputa" by Kathleen Williams. From Jonathan Swift and the Age of Compromise *(Lawrence, Kansas: University of Kansas Press, 1958), pp. 165–77. Copyright © 1958 by the University of Kansas Press. Reprinted by permission of the publisher.*

—even as to size—with William Gilbert's dipping-needle,[1] and though it uses Gilbert's idea "of the Earth's whole Body being but one great Magnet; and, lesser Magnets being so many Terrella's sympathising with the Whole," presents through this contemporary scientific interest a political philosophy and a comment on man's relation to nature which go beyond the merely topical: beyond particular scientific discoveries or the relation of the kingdoms of England and Ireland. The flying island, "the King's Demesn," in its devious and sensitive oblique movements, suggests the relationship of king and country. Laputa is ultimately dependent upon Balnibarbi, its motions only allowed by the magnetic quality of the "King's Dominions." It is this quality which has allowed the Laputan king to establish his power over the fixed land, but there is a reciprocal dependence, for if either side pressed its power too far the result would be general ruin. The King's last resource, in case of defiance from the populace of Balnibarbi, is to let the flying island drop upon their heads, but this, though it would certainly destroy both houses and men, would at the same time damage the adamant of Laputa itself. . . . As for the nobles and ministers, they are in part committed to the welfare of both lands, for while they attend at the Laputan court their estates lie on the continent below, so that they will never dare advise the King to make himself "the most absolute Prince in the Universe" by so ruthless and desperate a course. The balance of power, and the delicate relationships which subsist between a monarch and those whom he governs, could scarcely be better represented than by conditions in Laputa and Balnibarbi, and it is typical of Swift that these relationships, though given a color of respect for human life and liberties, are seen to be really dependent upon the exact adjustment of practical necessities; the self-love of each party is carried as far as it can go without that open conflict with the self-love of others which would bring it to destruction.

Further, the relation of the greater and lesser magnets, Laputa and Balnibarbi, suggests the limited usefulness of that understanding of the laws of the universe upon which the Newtonian era so prided itself, and which is one of the main objects of Swift's satiric comment in this book. The Laputan king, for all his knowledge of cosmic circumstance, for all the ingenuity of his flying island, is yet dependent upon the firm earth beneath him for every movement Laputa can make; for all his theoretic achievement man is, in practice, dependent upon and circumscribed by other men and by laws of nature, of which he can take a certain limited advantage but which he can neither alter nor, finally, explain. The astronomers of Laputa, although they have

[1] M. H. Nicolson and N. M. Mohler, "Swift's 'Flying Island' in the Voyage to Laputa," *Annals of Science,* 2 (1937).

written "large Systems concerning the Stone" whose movements control the course of the flying island, can give no better reason for the
inability of Laputa to rise above four miles, or to move beyond the
extent of the King's continental dominions, than the self-evident one
"That the Magnetick Virtue does not extend beyond the Distance of
four Miles, and that the Mineral which acts upon the Stone in the
Bowels of the Earth, and in the Sea about Six Leagues distant from
the Shoar, is not diffused through the whole Globe, but terminated with
the Limits of the King's Dominions." [2] Their pursuit of second causes
ends in inscrutable mystery, which their confident exposition can only
conceal, not clarify. The allegory of Laputa and of Balnibarbi, "controlled by that which it alone controls," is indeed an epitome of the
situation more fully explored in the detailed descriptions of the inhabitants of the flying island and of conditions on the mainland below; the neat, generalized relationships help us to find our way in the
confusion of the Academy of Projectors and the alien clarities of the
Laputan court.

The Laputans, though they are in human shape, are more obviously
allegorical creatures than any in *Gulliver's Travels*. Their physical
characteristics express their nature as do those of the Brobdingnagians
or the Yahoos, but in a different way. Their effect is made, not through
exaggeration or isolation, but through distortion, of the physical, and
though by this means much of the force of Swift's greatest figures is
lost, this is in itself part of the meaning, since the Laputans have indeed lost their human quality in their abnormal absorption in things
remote from the concerns of men. They make little physical effect
upon us, for their outer aspect is as unnatural, as purely emblematic,
as that of a personification like Spenser's Occasion: "One of their Eyes
turned inward, and the other directly up to the Zenith" [3] because
they are completely absorbed in their own speculations and in the
study of the stars. Their interests are entirely abstract, and they see
nothing of the everyday practical world, ignoring the knowledge of
the senses as totally as Jack or the philosopher of *A Tale of a Tub*. The
Laputan is "always so wrapped up in Cogitation, that he is in manifest
Danger of falling down every Precipice, and bouncing his Head against
every Post; and in the Streets, of jostling others, or being jostled himself into the Kennel." [4] Because they scorn the evidence of the senses,
the Laputans are necessarily "very bad Reasoners," [5] though very positive and dogmatic ones, for the senses are "so many Avenues to the
Fort of Reason," which in them as in the mechanical operators of the

[2] *Works*, XI, 154 [in the Davis-Williams ed., 1941. Bk. III, ch. 3].
[3] XI, 143 [Bk. III, ch. 2].
[4] XI, 144 [Bk. III, ch. 2].
[5] XI, 147 [Bk. III, ch. 2].

spirit is wholly blocked up. These strange figures are akin not only to the mechanical operators but more closely to the spider-like world-makers. Like the author of *A Tale of a Tub,* they are less consistent than inclusive, summing up various departures from the middle way. One eye looks outward, but only to a remote world of abstractions where, in the regular motions of the heavens, mathematics and music join. One eye looks inward, to the mind where systems are spun out of a "Native Stock," not built up from that basis of observed fact which, however faulty our senses, is yet the only material upon which our reason can work constructively and practically. Laputan thinking produces results as flimsy and useless as a cobweb—Gulliver's ill-fitting suit, the devastated countryside of Balnibarbi.

The King and his court are devoted entirely to two subjects, music and mathematics, the most abstract of sciences. There is a topical reference, in that an interest in these "two eternal and immutable verities" and in the analogies between them serves to identify the Laputans as members of the Royal Society, but for centuries an interest in the relationship of mathematics and music had existed, so that it was by no means an exclusively contemporary concern. In the Middle Ages music, regarded as a mathematical science, had been one of the purest embodiments of unchanging law, and the Laputans with their absorption in music, mathematics, and astronomy, represent specifically the members of the Royal Society but more generally all those who believe that, by turning away from the impressions of the senses and the ordinary concerns of human nature they can ignore sublunary confusion and reach eternal truth. Swift's reference to the music of the spheres emphasizes this more general meaning; the Laputans spend hours at their instruments, preparing themselves to join in the music of the spheres, which they claim to be able to hear. Since mankind is traditionally deaf to this music because of the grossness of the senses through sin, the claim implies that the Laputans believe themselves to have escaped from such tyranny. To their impracticality is added the presumption of ignoring the inherited wisdom which sees man as a fallen creature separated, through his own fault, from the order, truth, and justice figured in the celestial harmony of the nine enfolded spheres.

The narrowness, even to inhumanity, of the Laputans is indeed stressed throughout. They have cut themselves off completely from all that is humanly creative and constructive. Even their food approaches as nearly as possible to the rarefied atmosphere in which they live, for their meat is carved into geometrical shapes and their poultry trussed up "into the Form of Fiddles." [6] Nor have they any conception of

[6] XI, 145 [Bk. III, ch. 2].

physical or sensuous beauty, since they see beauty only in mathematical
abstractions, and judge not by sense impressions but by an arbitrary
relation of animal forms to abstract shapes existing in their minds: "If
they would, for Example, praise the Beauty of a Woman, or any other
Animal, they describe it by Rhombs, Circles, Parallelograms, Ellipses,
and other Geometrical Terms; or else by Words of Art drawn from
Musick . . . the whole Compass of their Thoughts and Mind, being
shut up within the two forementioned Sciences." [7] But the world of
human beings cannot be adequately dealt with in mathematical terms,
and their wives, as a consequence, have fallen into matter, escaping
whenever possible into a life altogether physical and degraded, as
exaggeratedly animal as that of their husbands is exaggeratedly intellectual. The King has no interest in "the Laws, Government, History, Religion, or Manners of the Countries" [8] Gulliver has visited, and
his realm of Balnibarbi is chaotic. Gulliver "could not discover one
Ear of Corn, or Blade of Grass" [9] except in a few places, during his
journeys, and our minds revert to the kingdom of Brobdingnag, the
land which has been called a "simple Utopia of abundance," where
government is conducted with practical good will and a due regard
for traditional wisdom, and where the King regards his task as one of
promoting increase and life, making "two Ears of Corn, or two Blades
of Grass, to grow where only one grew before." The Laputans, on the
other hand, produce a world of death, and the results of their efforts
are purely destructive because their aims are impossibly high and are
unrelated to real conditions. Some day, they say, "a Palace may be
built in a Week, of Materials so durable as to last for ever without
repairing. All the Fruits of the Earth shall come to Maturity at whatever Season we think fit to chuse, and increase an Hundred Fold more
than they do at present; with innumerable other happy Proposals." [10]
In the meantime, houses are ruined, land uncultivated, and people
starving, and the only result of Laputan enterprise on the prosperous
estate of the old-fashioned Lord Munodi has been to destroy the mill
which had long provided his family and tenants, in order to make way
for one which should, on scientific principles, be better, but which
somehow fails to work. . . . That Munodi, the one successful land-
owner in Balnibarbi, should be a traditionalist is only to be expected;
"being not of an enterprizing Spirit, he was content to go on in the
old Forms; to live in the Houses his Ancestors had built, and act as
they did in every Part of Life without Innovation." [11]

[7] XI, 147 [Bk. III, ch. 2].
[8] XI, 150 [Bk. III, ch. 2].
[9] XI, 159 [Bk. III, ch. 4].
[10] XI, 161 [Bk. III, ch. 4].
[11] XI, 161 [Bk. III, ch. 4].

The activities of the members of the Academy of Projectors, though they involve experiment, are yet related to the abstract thinking of the King. For the most part, they are based on some wrongheaded abstract conception, and are really examples of what Pope calls reasoning downward, taking "the High Priori Road"; they are aspects, therefore, of the great modern heresy of ignoring "the old Forms" and relying on a spider-like spinning of thought. By blending experiment and High Priori reasoning in the Academy at Lagado, Swift is able to show scientific "projects" as yet another example of that whole development of thinking which leads away from the ways of a Christian and humanist tradition, and Pope's lines would refer as well to the mathematicians of Laputa and the scientists of Lagado as they do to Hobbes, Descartes, Spinoza, and Samuel Clarke:

> Let others creep by timid steps, and slow,
> On plain Experience lay foundations low,
> By common sense to common knowledge bred,
> And last, to Nature's Cause through Nature led.[12]

Indeed one of the projects is an exact allegorical equivalent of the process of reasoning downward to, instead of upward from, the foundations of plain experience: "There was a most ingenious Architect who had contrived a new Method for building Houses, by beginning at the Roof, and working downwards to the Foundation; which he justified to me by the like Practice of those two prudent Insects the Bee and the Spider." [13] We are not told the result of this method, but in other cases the ideas of the projectors do not well stand up to experiment; for instance, the notion of "plowing the Ground with Hogs to save the Charges of Plows, Cattle, and Labour" results, "upon Experiment," in no crop and a great deal of trouble and expense.

The experiments and their results allow Swift to collect together various images which, as so often, express his meaning through producing a certain atmosphere which must affect our response to Laputa and Balnibarbi. These projects leave an impression of uselessness, dirt, ephemerality, or death; the Academicians present for our inspection a spider web, a hog rooting up acorns, a muddle of painters' colors, a dead dog. Their efforts are summed up in an illustrious member who has been given the title of "the Universal Artist," and who has been for thirty years directing his followers in various ways of converting things into their opposites, thus turning the useful into the unusable and the vital into the atrophied. Air is made tangible and marble soft, land is sown with chaff and naked sheep are bred; and perhaps most

[12] *The Dunciad*, IV, 465–68.
[13] XI, 164 [Bk. III, ch. 5].

exact of all as an epitome of the achievements of the Academy, the
hooves of a living horse are being petrified. The projects of Lagado
are, in fact, conducted in an atmosphere similar to that of *A Tale of a
Tub,* an atmosphere of aimless activity, distorted values, and a perversion of things from their proper purpose even to the point of removing
all life and meaning from them. The results produced are woolless
sheep, dead dogs, horses whose living hooves are turned to stone. The
mechanism of the *Tale* exists in Lagado too, in the machine which is
to replace the thinking and creating mind of man and will, by pure
chance, eventually produce "Books in Philosophy, Poetry, Politicks,
Law, Mathematicks and Theology." [14] While the prevailing effect of
the images we associate with Lilliput and, especially, Brobdingnag is
of man and other animals as vigorous physical presences, the effect
of Laputa and its subject kingdom is of a wilful abandoning of the
physical and of the vital for the abstract, the mechanical, and the
unproductive. The prevailing images here are not of real people and
animals, even "little odious vermin," but of ruins, mechanical constructions, men who look like allegorical figures and women who are
thought of as rhomboids or parallelograms. Animals are only negatively
present, as in the pathetic horses and sheep of the Academy. Even
Laputa itself is a mechanical device, and the flying island expresses
not only the Laputans' desertion of the common earth of reality but
their conversion of the universe to a mechanism and of living to a
mechanical process.

From Lagado Gulliver makes his way to Glubbdubdrib, where again
he is in a world of no-meaning, of delusion and death, darker and
more shadowy than Laputa. In the palace of the sorcerer who is gover-
nor of the island he has a series of singularly uninformative inter-
views with the ghosts of the famous dead, and Alexander and Hannibal,
who as conquerors and destroyers had little to recommend them to
Swift, make particularly trivial replies. We are given a gloomy enough
picture of both the ancient and the modern world, and upon this
ghostly history follows the most somber episode of all, that of the
Struldbrugs of Luggnagg, in which the lesson of Laputa with its naïve
hopes, its misplaced ambition, and its eventual sterility is repeated with
more open seriousness. A right sense of values, a proper attitude to
living, is here suggested not through the handling of contemporary
aims and habits of thought but through the figure of man, immortal
yet still painfully recognizable, and perhaps owing some of its power
and poignancy to Swift's own fear of death and, still more, of decay, of
a lingering old age giving way at last to helpless lunacy. Gulliver,
hearing of the immortals, cries out "as in a Rapture," exclaiming upon

[14] XI, 166 [Bk. III, ch. 5].

the wisdom and happiness which they must have achieved. They must, he says, "being born exempt from that universal Calamity of human Nature, have their Minds free and disingaged, without the Weight and Depression of Spirits caused by the continual Apprehension of Death," [15] and he is only too willing to tell his hearers how he would plan his life, if he were a Struldbrug, to bring the greatest possible benefit to himself and his country. In fact, of course, the immortal and aged creatures, though free from the fear of death, are yet as full of fears and wretchedness as any other men: being what we are, we will always find occasion to display those vices which as human beings we will always have, however long we may live. The Struldbrugs certainly do not keep their minds free and disengaged, and for them the prospect of endless life does not conjure up visions of endless improvement in wisdom and virtue. They regard their immortality as a "dreadful Prospect" even as other men regard their death, and indeed they long to die as did the wretched Sibyl in Petronius's *Satyricon,* regarding with great jealousy those of their acquaintance who go "to an Harbour of Rest, to which they themselves never can hope to arrive." [16] Immortal man is still man, limited in his capacity for growth, sinful, fearful, dissatisfied; the somber simplicity of the passage, and indeed of the whole of the visit to Glubbdubdrib, is reminiscent of Johnson's methods rather than of Swift's, and the message is essentially similar. Gulliver, who has dreamed of being a king, a general, or a great lord, and now dreams of being a Struldbrug, has to learn the same lesson as the Prince of Abyssinia: that life is a serious, difficult, and above all a moral undertaking, that whatever excuses we may find for ourselves, however we may dream of the greatness we could have achieved under other conditions, we will realize at last that humanity is always the same, and that there is no escape from our vices and our trivialities. Gulliver says that he grew "heartily ashamed of the pleasing Visions I had formed; and thought no Tyrant could invent a Death into which I would not run with Pleasure from such a Life," [17] and that he would have been willing, if it had not been forbidden by the laws of Luggnagg, to send a couple of Struldbrugs to England to arm the people against that fear of death which is natural to mankind.

So the "Voyage to Laputa," which opens among a people essentially frivolous in its refusal to face the facts of human existence, ends face to face with inescapable reality. Laputa, where the search for the clarity of abstractions involves such confusion in the living world, seems at first merely hilarious and absurd, but as confusion turns to

[15] XI, 192 [Bk. III, ch. 10].
[16] XI, 196 [Bk. III, ch. 10].
[17] XI, 198 [Bk. III, ch. 10].

mechanism and destruction, this remoteness and unreality becomes not only ludicrous but evil, and the countries about Laputa and Balnibarbi are seen to be places of superstition, sorcery, and tyranny, of ghosts and the corpselike immortals of Luggnagg. The voyage to illusion, the escape from facts, ends in a darker reality than any Gulliver has yet encountered. Gulliver himself, in this book, becomes a part of the world of illusion and distorted values. Already in the earlier voyages the shifting, inconsistent quality which Gulliver shares with all Swift's satiric mouthpieces has been made to contribute to effects of relativity, and to suggest the hold of physical circumstances over mankind. That he is, generally, a different man in Brobdingnag and in Lilliput is made into part of Swift's presentation of human nature. In the "Voyage to Laputa," any still surviving notion that Gulliver is a safe guide through these strange countries is ended. He ceases to have any character and, in effect, vanishes, so that for the most part the satire speaks directly to us; the "mouthpiece" performs no real function. The transparent account of "Tribnia, by the Natives called Langden," where "the Bulk of the People consisted wholly of Discoverers, Witnesses, Informers, Accusers, Prosecutors, Evidences, Swearers," [18] owes nothing to Gulliver, and would be quite inconceivable from what we have known of him before; in the second voyage he had "wished for the Tongue of Demosthenes or Cicero, that might have enabled me to celebrate the Praise of my own dear native Country in a Style equal to its Merits and Felicity." [19] Here he is being frankly used for ironic comment, as his exaggerated enthusiasm shows; in the description of Tribnia, he is not being used at all. From time to time he is given a momentary reality, but of the most perfunctory kind; there is no attempt to endow him even with the one or two dominant characteristics that he is given elsewhere. His approval of projects, or his tendency to dream about impossible situations instead of getting on with the business of living, his dismissal of obviously desirable political reforms as "wild impossible Chimaeras," are, quite openly, mentioned for satiric purposes of a very simple kind. The handling of Gulliver is in fact far less interesting, and his contribution is far slighter, than in any other book, probably because his function had been worked to its limits in the voyages already written, which included the "Voyage to the Houyhnhnms." But whether or not Swift planned it so, Gulliver's virtual lack of function, indeed of existence, in the "Voyage to Laputa" has a certain effectiveness in contributing to the atmosphere of meaningless activity and self-deceit, leading to a shadowy despair. The gradual undermining of the comparatively solid worlds of Lilliput and

[18] XI, 175 [Bk. III, ch. 6].
[19] XI, 111 [Bk. II, ch. 6].

Brobdingnag was achieved partly through a shift in Gulliver's position; here he merges completely into his surroundings, and serves merely to describe what he sees, so that we cannot take him seriously as an interpreter. When he reappears in Book IV, we are well prepared to find that his function will not be a simple one either of sensible comment on the vagaries of a strange country, or of admiration for a Utopia, for we have accepted him as one of the many figures in the *Travels,* expressing meaning by his relationship to them, and no more exempt than they from satiric treatment. As a completion of the processes begun in Lilliput and Brobdingnag, and as a preparation for the resolution in Houyhnhnmland, the Laputan voyage performs its task adequately, though without the formal elegance and neatness of the other books.

The Pride of Lemuel Gulliver

by Samuel H. Monk

Gulliver's Travels is a complex book. It is, of course, a satire on four aspects of man: the physical, the political, the intellectual, and the moral. The last three are inseparable, and when Swift writes of one he always has in view the others. It is also a brilliant parody of travel literature; and it is at once science fiction and a witty parody of science fiction. It expresses savage indignation at the follies, vices, and stupidities of men, and everywhere implicit in the book as a whole is an awareness of man's tragic insufficiency. But at the same time it is a great comic masterpiece, a fact that solemn and too-sensitive readers often miss.

A friend once wrote me of having shocked an associate by remarking that he had laughed often on rereading *Gulliver's Travels*. "What should I have done?" he asked me. "Blown out my brains?" I am sure that Swift would have approved my friend's laughter. To conclude that *Gulliver's Travels* expresses despair or that its import is nihilistic is radically to misread the book. All of Swift's satire was written in anger, contempt, or disgust, but it was written to promote self-knowledge in the faith that self-knowledge will lead to right action. Nothing would have bewildered him more than to learn that he had led a reader to the desperate remedy of blowing out his brains. But the book is so often called morbid, so frequently have readers concluded that it is the work of an incipient madman, that I think it worth while to emphasize the gayety and comedy of the voyages as an indication of their author's essential intellectual and spiritual health. True, seventeen years after finishing *Gulliver's Travels,* Swift was officially declared *non compos mentis*. But his masterpiece was written at the height of his powers, and the comic animation of the book as a whole rules out the suspicion of morbidity and mental illness.

We laugh and were meant to laugh at the toy kingdom of the Lilliputians; at the acrobatic skill of the politicians and courtiers; at the absurd jealousy of the diminutive minister who suspects an adul-

From "The Pride of Lemuel Gulliver" by Samuel H. Monk. From the Sewanee Review, *63 (1955), 48–71. Copyright © 1955 by the University of the South. Reprinted by permission of the editor.*

terous relationship between his wife and the giant Gulliver. We laugh at the plight of Gulliver in Brobdingnag: one of the lords of creation, frightened by a puppy, rendered ludicrous by the tricks of a mischievous monkey, in awe of a dwarf; embarrassed by the lascivious antics of the maids of honor; and at last content to be tended like a baby by his girl-nurse. We laugh at the abstractness of the philosophers of Laputa, at the mad experimenters of Balnibarbi. And I am sure that we are right in at least smiling at the preposterous horses, the Houyhnhnms, so limited and so positive in their knowledge and opinions, so skilled in such improbable tasks as threading needles or carrying trays, so complacent in their assurance that they are "the Perfection of Nature." Much of the delight that we take in *Gulliver's Travels* is due to this gay, comic, fanciful inventiveness. Swift might well say in the words of Hamlet: "Lay not that flattering unction to your soul/That not your trespass but my madness speaks." Swift did not wish us to blow out our brains; he did wish us to laugh. But beyond the mirth and liveliness are gravity, anger, anxiety, frustration—and he meant us to experience them fully.

For there is an abyss below this fantastic world—the dizzying abyss of corrupt human nature. Swift is the great master of shock. With perfect control of tone and pace, with perfect timing, he startles us into an awareness of this abyss and its implications. We are forced to gaze into the stupid, evil, brutal heart of humanity, and when we do, the laughter that Swift has evoked is abruptly silenced. The surface of the book is comic, but at its center is tragedy, transformed through style and tone into icy irony. Soft minds have found Swift's irony unnerving and depressing and, in self-protection, have dismissed him as a repellent misanthrope. Stronger minds that prefer unpalatable truths to euphoric illusions have found this irony bracing and healthful. . . .

The first character to demand our attention is Gulliver himself. He is the narrator, the principal actor. We see through his eyes, feel his feelings, share his thoughts. We are in his company from first to last, and it is important that we come to know him as quickly as possible. What is he like and what is his role in the book? He is first of all a bit of a bore, for his mind is irritatingly circumstantial and unimaginative: observe the numerous insignificant biographical details which he gives us in the first pages of the book. Gradually, however, we come to like him and to enjoy his company. In all respects he is an average good man. He has had some university education both at Cambridge and at Leyden, where he studied medicine. He is observant (and we eventually come to be grateful for his gift of close observation and circumstantial reporting, once he has something worth observing and reporting), reasonably intelligent, thoroughly capable in an emergency, and both brave and hopeful. If he lacks imagination and inventiveness, so much the better; for we can be sure that what he tells us, no matter how strange, is true. He is simple, direct, uncomplicated. At the outset he is full of naive good will, and, though he grows less naive and more critical as a result of his voyaging among remote nations, he retains his benevolence throughout the first three voyages. It is a pity that so fine an example of the bluff, good-natured, honest Englishman should at last grow sick and morbid and should be driven mad— but that, I am afraid, is what befalls him.

All of this Gulliver is; but let us notice carefully what he is NOT. He is NOT Jonathan Swift. The meaning of the book is wholly distorted if we identify the Gulliver of the last voyage with his creator, and lay Gulliver's misanthropy at Swift's door. He is a fully rendered, objective, dramatic character, no more to be identified with Swift than Shylock is to be identified with Shakespeare. This character acts and is acted upon; he changes, he grows in the course of his adventures. Like King Lear, he begins in simplicity, grows into sophistication, and ends in madness. Unlike King Lear he is never cured.

The four voyages "into several remote nations of the world," are so arranged as to attain a climactic intensification of tone as we travel through increasing darkness into the black heart of humanity. But the forward movement is interrupted by the third voyage, a macabre scherzo on science, politics, economics as they are practiced by madmen—Swift's term for those who misuse and abuse human reason. Observe that the tone of each voyage is established by the nature of the event that brings about the adventure: in the first voyage (the most benign and the gayest) accident, or at worst, the carelessness of the lookout, accounts for the shipwreck; in the second, much more savage in tone, Gulliver is left alone in a strange land, through the cowardice of his shipmates; in the third, he is captured and later abandoned by pirates (evil in action); in the fourth, his crew of cutthroats mutinies, seizes the ship, and leaves him to starve on a near-by island. . . .

It is best to consider the first two voyages together and to notice how effectively Swift uses the idea of the great chain of being. Pascal, writing of man's disproportion, had asked: "For in fact, what is man in nature? A nothing in comparison with the Infinite, an All in comparison with the Nothing, a mean between nothing and everything." Swift transposes this theme into another key, and makes it the major instrument of his satire. In the first two voyages, Gulliver is made aware of his disproportion; placed on this isthmus of a middle state, in the voyage to Lilliput he looks down the chain of being and knows himself an awkward, if kindly, giant in that delicate kingdom; in the voyage to Brobdingnag he looks up the chain and discovers a race of "superior beings," among whom his pride shrivels through the humiliating knowledge of his own physical insignificance. The emphasis here is upon size, the physical; but it is none the less notable that Lilliputia calls into operation Gulliver's engaging kindliness and gentleness, and that Brobdingnag brings out his moral and physical courage. Though comically and tragically disproportioned, man has moral virtues which he can and does exercise.

But Swift's satire is a two-edged sword. What of the inhabitants of these strange lands? They too are disproportioned. From the start the Lilliputians win our interest and liking: these pigmies ingeniously capture the Hercules whom chance has cast on their shore; they humanely solve the problem of feeding him; their pretty land and their fascinating little city take our fancy. But in the end what do they prove to be? prideful, envious, rapacious, treacherous, cruel, vengeful, jealous, and hypocritical. Their primitive social and political systems have been corrupted; they are governed by an Emperor who is ambitious totally to destroy the neighboring kingdom, and by courtiers and ministers who are chosen not for their fitness for office, but for their skill in walking the tightrope, leaping over sticks or creeping under them. "Climbing," Swift once remarked, "is performed in the same Posture with Creeping." These little people, like Gulliver himself, are an instance of the disproportion of man. Their vices, their appetites, their ambitions, their passions are not commensurate with their tiny stature. They appear to Gulliver as he and his kind must appear to the higher orders of beings—as venomous and contemptibly petty.

In Brobdingnag we meet creatures ten times the size of Europeans, and we share Gulliver's anxiety lest their moral natures be as brutish as their bodies. But the reverse is true; and through a violent and effective shift of symbol, tone, and point of view, Gulliver, who seemed lovable and humane among the Lilliputians, appears an ignominious and morally insensitive being in contrast to the enlightened and benevolent Brobdingnagians. Since Gulliver is we, his shame, insufficiency, and ludicrousness are ours.

When the peasants discover him, they feel both curiosity and repulsion: the farmer picks him up "with the Caution of one who endeavours to lay hold on a small dangerous Animal in such a Manner that it shall not be able either to scratch or to bite him, . . ." [1] Gulliver fears that his captor may dash him to the ground, "as we usually do any little hateful Animal which we have a Mind to destroy." The change in tone and intent is obvious.

Gulliver is submitted to one humiliation after another, but he is still capable of a fatuous blindness to the defects of European society,

[1] [Bk. II, ch. 1.]

and when the King questions him about England, he describes with
uncritical enthusiasm its class system, its constitution, its laws, its
military glory, and its history. In the questions which the king asks
and which Gulliver meets with only an embarrassed silence, the voice
of morality is heard condemning the institutions of the modern world.
And the verdict of a moral being on European man is given in words
as icy as controlled contempt can make them: "But, by what I have
gathered from your own Relation, and the Answers I have with much
Pains wringed and extorted from you; I cannot but conclude the Bulk
of your Natives to be the most pernicious Race of little odious Vermin
that Nature ever suffered to crawl upon the Surface of the Earth." [2]

Such a conclusion is inevitable, for the King is high-minded, benevolent, and, in Swift's sense of the word, rational: i.e., he and his people
think practically, not theoretically; concretely, not metaphysically;
simply, not intricately. Brobdingnag is a Swiftian Utopia of common
good sense and morality; and Gulliver, conditioned by the corrupt
society from which he comes, appears naive, blind, and insensitive to
moral values. His account of the history of England in the seventeenth
century evokes the King's crushing retort:

> . . . it was only an Heap of Conspiracies, Rebellions, Murders, Massacres,
> Revolutions, Banishments; the very worst Effects that Avarice, Faction,
> Hypocracy, Perfidiousness, Cruelty, Rage, Madness, Hatred, Envy, Lust,
> Malice, and Ambition could produce.[3]

Notice the carefully arranged disorder of that list, the calculated
avoidance of climax. This is a favorite device of Swift: the irrational,
the appetitive, the evil nature of man *is* disorder.

The King is horrified when Gulliver offers him a way to complete
dominion over his subjects by teaching him to make gunpowder. And
Gulliver, speaking as a European, feels contemptuous surprise: "A
strange Effect of *narrow Principles* and *short Views!*" The King is
baffled by the concept of political *science*—how can the *art* of government be reduced to a science?

> He confined the knowledge of governing within very *narrow Bounds;*
> to common Sense and Reason, to Justice and Lenity, to the Speedy
> Determination of Civil and criminal Causes; with some other obvious
> Topicks which are not worth considering. And he gave it for his
> Opinion; that whoever could make two Ears of Corn, or two Blades of
> Grass to grow upon a Spot of Ground where only one grew before
> would deserve better of Mankind, and do more essential Service to his
> Country, than the whole Race of Politicians put together.[4]

[2] [Bk. II, ch. 6.]
[3] [Bk. II, ch. 6.]
[4] [Bk. II, ch. 7.]

The learning of the Brobdingnagians is simple and practical, "consisting only in Morality, History, Poetry, and Mathematicks." [5] Observe that Swift omits metaphysics, theoretical science, and theology from the category of useful knowledge.

Swift's attack on pride in the first two voyages is made more powerful because of his brilliant use of the chain of being. In so far as we recognize ourselves in the Lilliputians or in Gulliver in Brobdingnag, we become aware of our pettiness—of the disproportion of our race and of the shocking difference between what we profess and what we are. But Swift uses the good giants to strike an unexpected blow at human vanity and to introduce a motif which he employed with deadly effect in the last voyage. That motif is disgust, of which, as T. S. Eliot has remarked, he is the great master. Philosophers of the century were never tired of admiring the beautiful perfection of the human body, its intricateness, its perfect articulation, its happy appropriateness to the particular place that men occupy in the scheme of things. But how does this glorious body appear to lesser creatures—say to an insect? Swift forces us to answer by making us share Gulliver's disgust at the cancerous breasts and lousy bodies of the beggars; at the blotched color, the huge pores, the coarse hairs, and the nauseous odors of the maids of honor. Such is the skin, presumably, that the Brobdingnagians love to touch. Our beauty is only apparent; our disproportion is real.

The third voyage has always been considered the least successful; that may well be, but it is none the less interesting. Structurally it is loosely episodic, lacking unity of action and tone. Into it Swift seems to have put all the material that he could not work into the other three voyages. It is a fantasia on two themes which Swift treats under a single metaphor: the metaphor is science, the themes are politics and the abuse of reason. In short, the voyage is a digression on madness, on the divorce of man and good sense in the modern world. . . .

The climactic fourth voyage is the great section of *Gulliver's Travels*. It has provoked violent attacks on Swift and his book, entirely, I think, because it has been misunderstood. It has offended the unreflective and pious Christian, the sentimentalist, and the optimist. Thackeray, lecturing to the ladies in London in 1851, the year in which the Great Exhibition seemed to give the lie to every opinion that Swift held, may serve as an example, by no means unique, of the capacity of this voyage to shock. He advised his ladies not to read the last voyage, and to hoot the Dean. And the meaning that he found in it was "that man is utterly wicked, desperate, and imbecile, and his passions are monstrous, and his boasted power mean, that he is and deserves to be the shame of brutes, and ignorance is better than his

[5] [Bk. II, ch. 7.]

vaunted reason." "It is Yahoo language," he continues, "a monster gibbering shrieks and gnashing imprecations against mankind . . . filthy in word, filthy in thought, furious, raging, obscene."

The legend of Swift as a savage, mad, embittered misanthrope largely rests upon this wrong-headed, sensational reading of the last voyage. In my opinion the work is that of a Christian-humanist and a moralist who no more blasphemes against the dignity of human nature than do St. Paul and some of the angrier prophets of the Old Testament. Swift has been misunderstood for several reasons:

1. The sheer intensity and violent rhetoric of the voyage are overwhelming and may well numb the critical sense of certain readers.

2. Gulliver in the frenzy of his mad misanthropy has been too facilely identified with Swift. Gulliver speaks for Gulliver and not for his creator in the final pages of the book, and careful reading should reveal the plain fact that he becomes the victim of Swift's irony as he grows to hate the human race. The final pages of the book are grimly comic.

3. The primary symbols of the voyage have been totally misunderstood. The Houyhnhnms have been regarded as Swift's ideal for man, and the Yahoos have been identified as his representation of what men are. Neither of these opinions, I believe, is correct.

Let us begin with the Houyhnhnms and the Yahoos. In the first two voyages Gulliver is shown uncomfortably situated on the isthmus of a middle state between the very large and the very small. In this voyage he also stands on an isthmus, but now it is between the purely rational and the purely sensual—between Houyhnhnm and Yahoo. Neither of these symbols can stand for man, since Gulliver himself is the symbol of humanity. Unfortunately for poor Gulliver, he shares somehow in the nature of both extremes. Swift simply isolates the two elements that combine in the duality of man, the middle link, in order to allow Gulliver to contemplate each in its essence.

Does Swift recommend that Gulliver (who, remember, is we) should strive to become a Houyhnhnm? We discover that in every sense Houyhnhnmland is a rationalistic Utopia. The Houyhnhnms are the embodiment of pure reason. They know neither love nor grief nor lust nor ambition. They cannot lie; indeed they have no word for lying and are hard put to it to understand the meaning of *opinion*. Their society is an aristocracy, resting upon the slave labor of the Yahoos and the work of an especially-bred servant class. With icy, stoical calm they face the processes of life—marriage, childbirth, accident, death. Their society is a planned society that has achieved the mild anarchy that many Utopian dreamers have aspired to. They practice eugenics, and since they know no lust, they control the size of their population; children are educated by the state; their agrarian economy is supervised by a democratic council; government is entirely conducted by periodic assemblies. The Houyhnhnms feel natural human affection for each other, but they love every one equally. It is all very admirable, but it is remote from the possibilities of human life.

Does Swift intend us to accept this as his ideal way of life? He who loved and hated and fought and bled internally through *saeva indignatio*? I think not. The Houyhnhnms are obviously Cartesians and as obviously stoics. "Neither is *Reason* among them a Point problematical as with us," reports Gulliver, "where Men can argue with Plausibility on both Sides of a Question; but strikes you with immediate Conviction; . . ." [6] This is the Houyhnhnm version of Descartes' rational intuition of clear and distinct ideas. Now Swift was anti-Cartesian from his first published satire, for the simple reason that he held that Descartes was self-deluded and that man's reason was incapable of the feats that Descartes attributed to it. The Houyhnhnms are stoics, and Swift recorded his view of stoicism in *Thoughts on Various Subjects*: "The Stoical Scheme of supplying our Wants, by lopping off our Desires, is like cutting off our Feet when we want Shoes." It is Gulliver, not Swift, who is dazzled by the Houyhnhnms and who aspires to rise above the human condition and to become pure intelligence as these horses and the angels are.

The most powerful single symbol in all Swift is the Yahoos. They do not represent Swift's view of man, but rather of the bestial element in man—the unenlightened, unregenerate, irrational element in human nature—the id or the libido, if you will. Hence the Houyhnhnms classify Gulliver with them; hence the female Yahoo wishes to couple with him; hence despite his instinctive recoiling from them, Gulliver has to admit with shame and horror that he is more like them than he is like the Houyhnhnms. This I think is clear. Because of his neglect or misuse of human reason, European man has sunk nearer to the Yahoo pole of his nature than he has risen toward the Houyhnhnm pole. The seeds of human society and of human depravity, as they exist in Europe, are clearly discerned in the society and conduct of the Yahoos. Gulliver looks into the obscene abyss of human nature unlighted by the frail light of reason and of morality, and the sight drives him mad.

Repelled by what he sees, he, not Swift, identifies the Yahoos with man; and he, not Swift, turns misanthrope. Since he will not be a Yahoo, he seeks to become, as nearly as possible, a Houyhnhnm. But he can do so only by denying his place in and responsibility to the human condition, by aspiring above the middle link, which is man, to the next higher link, that of the purely rational. The wise Houyhnhnm, to whom he gives his terrifying account of European man and

[6] [Bk. IV, ch. 8.]

society, concludes that "the corruption of reason" is worse than brutality itself, and that man is more dangerous than the Yahoo. This is profoundly true. But its effect on Gulliver is to awaken loathing of all that is human.

Lear, gazing on the naked, shivering Edgar, disguised as a Tom o' Bedlam, cries: "Thou art the thing itself; unaccommodated man is no more but such a poor, bare, forked animal as thou art." And in that intense moment, he goes mad. Something of the same thing befalls Gulliver. He thinks he has seen the thing itself. Though the Houyhnhnms never acknowledge that he is more than an unusually gifted Yahoo, he aspires to their rationality, stoicism, and simple wisdom; and persuaded that he has attained them, he feeds his growing misanthropy on pride, which alienates him not only from his remote kinsmen, the Yahoos, but eventually from his brothers, the human race. . . .

From the moment that the banished Gulliver despairingly sets sail from Houyhnhnmland, his pride, his misanthropy, his madness are apparent. Deluded by his worship of pure reason, he commits the error of the Houyhnhnms in equating human beings with the Yahoos. Captured by a Portuguese crew and forced to return from sullen solitude to humanity, he trembles between fear and hatred. The captain of the ship, Don Pedro de Mendez, like Gulliver himself, shares the nature of the Houyhnhnm and the Yahoo; and like the Gulliver of the first voyage he is tolerant, sympathetic, kindly, patient, and charitable; but Gulliver can no longer recognize these traits in a human being. With the myopic vision of the Houyhnhnms, he perceives only the Yahoo and is repelled by Don Pedro's clothes, food, and odor. Gradually, however, he is nursed back to partial health, and is forced to admit in the very accent of his admired horses, that his benefactor has a "very good *human* Understanding." But the Gulliver who writes this book is still under the control of his *idée fixe,* and when we last see him he prefers the smell and conversation of his two horses to the company of his wife and children. This is misanthropy in Timon's manner, not Swift's. In the brilliant and intricately ironic coda with which the book ends, Swift directs his savage, comic gaze straight at Gulliver and his insane pretensions.

> My Reconcilement to the *Yahoo*-kind in general might not be so difficult, if they would be content with those Vices and Follies only which Nature hath entitled them to. I am not in the least provoked at the Sight of a Lawyer, a Pickpocket, a Colonel, a Fool, a Lord, a Gamester, a Politician, a Whoremunger, a Physician, an Evidence, a Suborner, an Attorney, a Traytor, or the like: This is all according to the due Course of Things: But when I behold a Lump of Deformity, and Diseases both of Body and Mind, smitten with *Pride,* it immediately breaks all the

Measures of my Patience; neither shall I ever be able to comprehend
how such an Animal and such a Vice could tally together.[7]

The grim joke is that Gulliver himself is the supreme instance of a
creature smitten with pride. His education has somehow failed. He
has voyaged into several remote nations of the world, but the journeys
were not long, because of course he has never moved outside the
bounds of human nature. The countries he visited, like the Kingdom
of Heaven, are all within us. The ultimate danger of these travels was
precisely the one that destroyed Gulliver's humanity—the danger that
in his explorations he would discover something that he was not
strong enough to face. This befell him, and he took refuge in a sick
and morbid pride that alienated him from his species and taught him
the gratitude of the Pharisee—"Lord, I thank Thee that I am not
as other men."

Swift himself, in his personal conduct, displayed an arrogant pride.
But he was never guilty of the angelic, dehumanizing pride of Gulliver,
who writes in a letter to his Cousin Sympson:

> I must freely confess, that since my last Return, some corruptions of
> my *Yahoo* Nature have revived in me by Conversing with a few of your
> Species, and particularly those of my own Family, by an unavoidable
> Necessity; else I should never have attempted so absurd a Project as
> that of reforming the *Yahoo* Race in this Kingdom; but, I have now
> done with all such visionary Schemes for ever.

Jonathan Swift was stronger and healthier than Lemuel Gulliver.
He hated the stupidity and the sinfulness and the folly of mankind.
He could not accept the optimistic view of human nature that the
philosophers of the Enlightenment proposed. And so he could exclaim
to his contemporaries: "O wicked and perverse generation!" But,
until he entered upon the darkness of his last years, he did not abandon
his fellow man as hopeless or cease to announce, however indirectly,
the dignity and worth of human kind.

[7] [Bk. IV, ch. 12.]

The Houyhnhnms, the Yahoos, and
the History of Ideas

by R. S. Crane

Whatever else may be true of the [Fourth] Voyage, it will doubtless be agreed that one question is kept uppermost in it from the beginning, for both Gulliver and the reader. This is the question of what sort of animal man, as a species, really is; and the point of departure in the argument is the answer to this question which Gulliver brings with him into Houyhnhnmland and which is also, we are reminded more than once, the answer which men in general tend, complacently, to give to it. Neither he nor they have any doubt that only man, among "sensitive" creatures, can be properly called "rational"; all the rest—whether wild or tame, detestable or, like that "most comely and generous" animal, the horse, the reverse of that—being merely "brutes," not "endued with reason." The central issue, in other words, is primarily one of definition: is man, or is he not, correctly defined as a "rational creature"? It is significant that Gulliver's misanthropy at the end is not the result of any increase in his knowledge of human beings in the concrete over what he has had before; it is he after all who expounds to his Houyhnhnm master all those melancholy facts about men's "actions and passions" that play so large a part in their conversations; he has known these facts all along, and has still been able to call himself a "lover of mankind." The thing that changes his love into antipathy is the recognition that is now forced upon him that these facts are wholly incompatible with the formula for man's nature which he has hitherto taken for granted—are compatible, indeed, only with a formula, infinitely more humiliating to human pride, which pushes man nearly if not quite over to the opposite pole of the animal world.

What brings about the recognition is, in the first place, the deeply disturbing spectacle of the Houyhnhnms and the Yahoos. I can find

"The Houyhnhnms, the Yahoos, and the History of Ideas" by R. S. Crane. From Reason and the Imagination, *ed. J. A. Mazzeo (New York: Columbia University Press, 1962), pp. 243–53. Copyright © 1962 by Columbia University Press. Reprinted by permission of the publisher.*

nothing in the text that forces us to look on these two sets of strange creatures in any other light than that in which Gulliver sees them— not, that is, as personified abstractions, but simply as two concrete species of animals: existent species for Gulliver, hypothetical species for us. The contrast he draws between them involves the same pair of antithetical terms (the one positive, the other privative) that he has been accustomed to use in contrasting men and the other animals. The essential character of the Houyhnhnms, he tells us, is that they are creatures "wholly governed by reason"; the essential character of the Yahoos is that "they are the most unteachable of brutes," without "the least tincture of reason." The world of animals in Houyhnhnm- land, in other words, is divided by the same basic differences as the world of animals in Europe. Only, of course—and it is the shock of this that prepares Gulliver for his ultimate abandonment of the definition of man he has started with—it is a world in which the normal distribution of species between "rational creatures" and ir- rational "brutes" is sharply inverted, with horses, whom he can't help admiring, in the natural place of men, and man-like creatures, whom he can't help abhorring, in the natural place of horses.

This is enough in itself to cause Gulliver to view his original formula for his own species, as he says, "in a very different light." But he is pushed much farther in the same misanthropic direction by the questions and comments of his Houyhnhnm master, acting as a kind of Socrates. What thus develops is partly a reduction to absurdity of man's "pretensions to the character of a rational creature" and partly a demonstration of the complete parity in essential nature be- tween men and the Houyhnhnmland Yahoos. There is of course one striking difference—unlike the Yahoos, men are after all possessed of at least a "small proportion," a "small pittance" of reason, some in greater degree than others. But I can see no clear signs in the text that this qualification is intended to set men apart as a third, or inter- mediate, species for either Gulliver or the reader. For what is basic in the new definition of man as a merely more "civilized" variety of Yahoo is the fundamentally irrational "disposition" which motivates his habitual behaviour; and in relation to that his "capacity for reason" is only an acquired attribute which he is always in danger of losing and of which, as Gulliver says, he makes no other use, generally speaking, than "to improve and multiply those vices" whereof his "brethren [in Houyhnhnmland] had only the share that nature allotted them."

It is clear what a satisfactory historical explanation of this line of argument in the Voyage would have to do. It would have to account for Swift's very patent assumption that there would be a high degree of satirical force, for readers in 1726, in a fable which began with the

notion that man is pre-eminently a "rational creature" and then proceeded to turn this notion violently upside down, and which, in doing
so, based itself on a division of animal species into the extremes of
"rational creatures" and irrational "brutes" and on the paradoxical
identification of the former with horses and of the latter with beings
closely resembling men. Was there perhaps a body of teaching, not so
far brought into the discussion of the Voyage but widely familiar at
the time, that could have supplied Swift with the particular scheme
of ideas he was exploiting here? I suggest that there was, and also
that there is nothing strange in the fact that it has been hitherto
overlooked by Swift's critics. For one principal medium through which
these ideas could have come to Swift and his readers—the only one, in
fact, I know of that could have given him all of them—was a body of
writings, mainly in Latin, which students of literature in our day
quite naturally shy away from reading: namely, the old-fashioned
textbooks in logic that still dominated the teaching of that subject
in British universities during the later seventeenth and early eighteenth centuries.[1]

It is impossible not to be impressed, in the first place, by the
prominence in these textbooks of the particular definition of man
which the Voyage sought to discredit. *Homo est animal rationale*:
no one could study elementary logic anywhere in the British Isles in
the generation before *Gulliver* without encountering this formula or
variations of it (e.g., *Nullus homo est irrationalis*) in his manuals
and the lectures he heard. It appears as the standard example of
essential definition in the great majority of logics in use during these
years at Oxford, Cambridge, and Dublin; and in most of those in
which it occurs, it is given without comment or explanation as the
obviously correct formula for man's distinctive nature, as if no one
would ever question that man is, uniquely and above all, a rational
creature. It is frequently brought in many times over, in various
contexts, in individual textbooks: I have counted a dozen or so occurrences of it in Milton's *Art of Logic,* and many times that number
in the *Institutionum logicarum . . . libri duo* of Franco Burgersdijck
(or Burgersdicius), which was one of the most widely used, and also
one of the longest lived, of all these writings—it appeared in 1626
and was still prescribed at Dublin when Edmund Burke went there
as a Junior Freshman in 1744. I shall have some more to say of
Burgersdicius, or "Burgy" as Burke called him, presently; but it is
worth noting that he provides us, in one passage, with the very
question on which much of the fourth Voyage was to turn, with the

[1] There are useful descriptions of many, though by no means all, of these in
Wilbur Samuel Howell, *Logic and Rhetoric in England, 1500–1700* (Princeton,
1956).

answer Swift was *not* to give to it: "Quærenti enim, Quale animal est homo? apposité respondetur, Rationale." [2]

Not only, however, was the definition omnipresent in these books, but there is some evidence that it was thought of, in Swift's time, as the special property of the academic logicians. Locke, for instance, calls it in his *Essay* "the ordinary Definition of the Schools," the "sacred Definition of *Animal Rationale*" of "the learned Divine and Lawyer"; it goes, he implies, with "this whole *Mystery* of *Genera* and *Species,* which make such a noise in the Schools, and are, with Justice, so little regarded out of them" (III.iii.10; vi.26; iii.9). And there are other later testimonies to the same effect; among them these opening lines of an anonymous poem of the period after *Gulliver,* once ascribed to Swift—"The Logicians Refuted":

> Logicians have but ill defin'd
> As rational, the human kind;
> Reason, they say, belongs to man,
> But let them prove it if they can.
> Wise Aristotle and Smiglesius,
> By ratiocinations specious,
> Have strove to prove with great precision,
> With definition and division,
> *Homo est ratione preditum;*
> But for my soul I cannot credit 'em.[3]

But the logicians had more to offer Swift than the great authority which they undoubtedly conferred on the definition "rational animal." They could have suggested to him also the basic principle on which the inverted animal world of Houyhnhnmland was constructed, and consequently the disjunction that operated as major premise in his argument about man. Whoever it was, among the Greeks, that first divided the genus "animal" by the differentiae "rational" and "irrational," there is much evidence that this antithesis had become a commonplace in the Greco-Roman schools long before it was taken up by the writer who did more than any one else to determine the context in which the definition *animal rationale* was chiefly familiar to Englishmen of Swift's time. This writer was the Neoplatonist Porphyry of the third century A.D., whose little treatise, the *Isagoge,* or introduction to the categories of Aristotle, became, as is well known, one of the great sources of logical theorizing and teaching from the time of Boethius until well beyond the end of the seventeenth century.

---

[2] ["Then being asked, what kind of animal is man? the appropriate answer is, rational."]

[3] *The Busy Body,* No. 5, October 18, 1759.

There is no point in going into the details of Porphyry's doctrine: what is important for our purpose here is the new sanction he gave to the older division of animal species through his incorporation of it into the general scheme of differentiae for the category of substance which was later known as the *arbor porphyriana* or Porphyry's tree, especially in the diagrams of it that became a regular feature of the more elementary textbooks. Here it is, set forth discursively, in the crabbed prose of Burgersdicius (I quote the English version of 1697, but the Latin is no better). In seeking the definition of man, he writes, we must first observe that

> Man is a Substance; but because an Angel is also a Substance; *That it may appear how Man differs from an Angel,* Substance ought to be divided into Corporeal and Incorporeal. A Man is a *Body,* an Angel *without a Body:* But a Stone also is a *Body:* That therefore a Man may be distinguished from a Stone, divide Bodily or Corporeal Substance into Animate and Inanimate, that is, *with or without a Soul.* Man is a Corporeal Substance Animate, Stone Inanimate. But Plants are also *Animate:* Let us divide therefore again Corporeal Substance Animate into *Feeling and void of Feeling.* Man feels, a Plant not: But a Horse *also feels,* and likewise other Beasts. Divide we therefore Animate Corporeal Feeling Substance into Rational and Irrational. Here therefore *are we to stand,* since it appears that every, and only Man *is Rational.*[4]

And there was, finally, one other thing in these logics that could have helped to shape Swift's invention in the fourth Voyage. In opposing man as the only species of "rational animal" to the brutes, Porphyry obviously needed a specific instance, parallel to man, of an "irrational" creature; and the instance he chose—there were earlier precedents for the choice[5]—was the horse. The proportion "rational" is to "irrational" as man is to horse occurs more than once in the *Isagoge*; and the juxtaposition, in the same context, of *homo* and *equus* was a frequently recurring cliché in his seventeenth-century followers, as in the passage in Burgersdicius just quoted: other species of brutes were occasionally mentioned, but none of them nearly so often. And any one who studied these books could hardly fail to remember a further point—that the distinguishing "property" of this favorite brute was invariably given as whinnying (*facultas hinniendi*); *equus,* it was said again and again, *est animal hinnibile.*

To most Englishmen of Swift's time who had read logic in their youth—and this would include nearly all generally educated men— these commonplaces of Porphyry's tree, as I may call them for short,

---

[4] *Monitio Logica: or, An Abstract and Translation of Burgersdicius his Logick* (London, 1697), pp. 13–14 (second pagination).
[5] E.g., Quintilian, *Institutio oratoria,* VII. iii. 3, 24.

were as familiar as the Freudian commonplaces are to generally educated people today, and they were accepted, for the most part, in an even less questioning spirit, so that it might well have occurred to a clever satirist then that he could produce a fine shock to his readers' complacency as human beings by inventing a world in which horses appeared where the logicians had put men and men where they had put horses, and by elaborating, through this, an argument designed to shift the position of man as a species from the *animal rationale* branch of the tree, where he had always been proudly placed, as far as possible over toward the *animal irrationale* branch, with its enormously less flattering connotations. But have we any warrant for thinking that this, or something like it, was what Swift actually had in mind? It is clearly possible to describe the Voyage as, in considerable part at least, an anti-Porphyrian satire in the genre of the poem I quoted from earlier, "The Logicians Refuted." But is there any evidence that Swift planned it as such?

That the Porphyrian commonplaces had been known to him in their full extent from his days at Trinity College in the early 1680s we can hardly doubt in view of the kind of education in logic he was exposed to there. Among the books which all Junior Freshmen at Dublin in those years were required to study or hear lectures on, we know of three in which the Porphyrian apparatus and examples had a prominent place: the *Isagoge* itself (which was prescribed by the statutes of the College to be read twice over during the year), the older logic of Burgersdicius, and the newer *Institutio logicae* of Narcissus Marsh. It is true that Swift, according to his own later statement, detested this part of the curriculum, and it is true that on one examination in his last year his mark in Philosophy was *Male* (he had a *Bene* in Greek and Latin). But this was an examination in the more advanced branches of the Aristotelian system, and it is likely that he had fared better in the earlier examination in logic, since he had evidently been allowed to proceed with his class. It is possible, moreover, to infer from his occasional use of logical terms in his later writings that, abhorrent as the subject was to him, the time he had been compelled to spend on it as a Junior Freshman was not a total loss. He at least remembered enough of it to allude familiarly in different places to such things as a "long sorites," "the first proposition of a hypothetical syllogism," and the fallacy of two middle terms in a single syllogism;[6] and if this was possible, there is good reason to suppose that he had not forgotten the much simpler Porphyrian points about genera, species, and definition,

[6] See John M. Bullitt, *Jonathan Swift and the Anatomy of Satire* (Cambridge, Mass., 1953), p. 73. Cf. also Swift, "A Preface to the B——p of S——m's Introduction," in *Works*, ed. by Temple Scott, III, 150.

"rational" versus "irrational" animals, men and horses which he had been introduced to at the same time.

The crucial question, however, is whether he had these notions of the logicians at all actively in mind when, in the 1720s, he conceived and wrote the "Voyage to the Houyhnhnms." And here it will be well to take a fresh look at the two much-quoted letters about _Gulliver's Travels_ which he sent to Pope in 1725, just after that work was completed. In the first of these, that of September 29, after having told Pope that his chief aim is "to vex the world rather than divert it" and that he hates and detests "that animal called man," he goes on to remark: "I have got materials towards a treatise proving the falsity of that definition _animal rationale,_ and to show it should be only _rationis capax._ Upon this great foundation of misanthropy, though not in Timon's manner, the whole building of my Travels is erected; and I never will have peace of mind till all honest men are of my opinion." In the second letter, that of November 26, he desires that Pope and "all my friends" will "take a special care that my disaffection to the world may not be imputed to my age, for I have credible witnesses . . . that it has never varied from the twenty-first to the f——ty-eighth year of my life." He then adds a passage which has been read as a retraction of the judgment on humanity expressed in the first letter, though the final sentence makes clear, I think, that it was not so intended:

> I tell you after all, that I do not hate mankind; it is _vous autres_ [i.e., Pope and Bolingbroke] who hate them, because you would have them reasonable animals, and are angry for being disappointed. I have always rejected that definition, and made another of my own. I am no more angry with ——— than I am with the kite that last week flew away with one of my chickens; and yet I was glad when one of my servants shot him two days after.

The casual references in both letters to "that definition"—_"animal rationale"_ and "reasonable animals"—which Swift tells Pope he has "always rejected" have usually been interpreted by modern critics as allusions to such contemporary philosophical or theological heresies (from Swift's point of view) as the "optimism" of Shaftesbury or the "rationalism" of Descartes and the Deists. It is surely, however, a much less far-fetched conjecture, especially in view of the familiar textbook Latin of the first letter, to see in "that definition" nothing other or more than the "sacred definition" of the logicians which he had had inflicted on him, by thoroughly orthodox tutors, in his undergraduate days at Dublin.

I find this explanation, at any rate, much harder to disbelieve than any other that has been proposed; and all the more so because of another passage in the first letter which is almost certainly reminiscent

of the Trinity logic course in the early 1680s. It is the famous sentence
—just before the allusion to "that definition *animal rationale*" and
leading on to it—in which Swift says: "But principally I hate and detest
that animal called man, although I heartily love John, Peter, Thomas,
and so forth." Now to any one at all widely read in the logic textbooks
of Swift's time two things about this sentence are immediately evident:
first, that the distinction it turns on is the distinction to be found in
nearly all these books between a species of animals and individual
members of that species; and second, that the names "John, Peter,
Thomas, and so forth" are wholly in line with one of the two main
traditions of names for individuals of the species man that had persisted
side by side in innumerable manuals of logic since the Middle Ages:
not, of course, the older tradition of classical names—Socrates, Plato,
Alexander, Caesar—but the new tradition (which I have noted first in
Occam, though it doubtless antedates him) that drew upon the list
of apostles—Peter, John, Paul, James, Thomas, in roughly that descending order of preference. (Other non-classical names, like Stephen,
Catharine, Charles, Richard, also appear, but much less frequently.)

We can go farther than this, however. For although all three of
Swift's names occur separately in divers texts (Thomas least often),
the combination "John, Peter, Thomas, and so forth" was an extremely
unusual one. I have met with it, in fact, in only one book before
1725; and I have examined nearly all the logics, both Latin and English, down to that date for which I can find any evidence that they
had even a minor circulation in Great Britain. The exception, however, is a book which Swift could hardly have escaped knowing as an
undergraduate, since it was composed expressly for the use of Trinity
College students by the then Provost and had just recently come "on
the course" when he entered the College in 1682—namely, the *Institutio
logicae*, already referred to, of Narcissus Marsh (Dublin, 1679: reissued
Dublin, 1681). Early in the book Marsh gives a full-page diagram of
Porphyry's tree, with its inevitable opposition of *animal–rationale–
homo* and *animal–irrationale–brutum*; and here, as *individua* under
homo, we find "Joannes, Petrus, Thomas, &c." And a little later in the
book the same names are repeated in the same order as individual
specimens of *homo* in Marsh's analytical table for the category *sub-
stantia.*

Was this combination of names, then, Marsh's invention? There
is one further circumstance which suggests that it may well have been.
We know from his own testimony, [7] as well as from internal evidence,

---

[7] See his preface "Ad lectorem" in the 1681 issue (it is missing from some copies
but can be found in the Cambridge University Library copy and in that belonging
to Archbishop Marsh's Library, Dublin); also the entry for December 20, 1690, in
his manuscript diary.

that the source on which he based the greater part of his Dublin logic of 1679 was his own revision, published at Oxford in 1678, of the *Manuductio ad logicam* of the early seventeenth-century Jesuit logician Philippe Du Trieu. Now of the two passages in the Dublin book that contain Swift's three names, the first—the diagram of Porphyry's tree—has no counterpart in the Oxford book of 1678, though it has in Du Trieu's original text, where the names are "Petrus" and "Joannes." It would seem likely, then, that Marsh first thought of the combination "John, Peter, Thomas, and so forth" when he revised his earlier revision of Du Trieu for his Trinity students in 1679; and this is borne out by what he did at the same time with the other passage —the table of substance. This he retained almost exactly as it had been in Du Trieu except for the names under *homo*: here, where in 1678 he had reprinted Du Trieu's "Stephanus, Johannes, Catharina, &c.," he now wrote "Johannes, Petrus, Thomas, &c." Which would seem to imply a certain sense of private property in these particular names in this particular combination.

It is somewhat hard, then, not to conclude that Swift was remembering Marsh's logic as he composed the sentence, in his letter to Pope, about "John, Peter, Thomas, and so forth." But if that is true, can there be much doubt, in view of the Porphyrian context in which these names appear in Marsh, as to what tradition of ideas was in his mind when he went on to remark, immediately afterwards, that "the great foundation of misanthropy" on which "the whole building" of his *Travels* rested was his proof—against Marsh and the other logicians he had been made to study at Trinity—of "the falsity of that definition *animal rationale*"? [8]

---

[8] Since this essay went to press I have discussed some further aspects of the subject in a brief article, "The Rationale of the Fourth Voyage," in *Gulliver's Travels: An Annotated Text with Critical Essays*, ed. by Robert A. Greenberg (New York, 1961), pp. 300–7, and in a review of two recent papers on Swift and the Deists, in *PQ*, XL (1961), 427–30.

Swift: Order and Obligation

by Martin Price

In *Gulliver's Travels* Swift carries the conflict of orders to its sharpest expression. Lemuel Gulliver is the most famous of Swift's masks or personae, and, as always, it is important to see these masks in their fictional integrity first of all. Swift may not be consistent in maintaining them; they become at moments transparencies through which his irony shines in full intensity, but much of the nonsense that has been written about Swift's works derives from a failure to observe the character of their spokesmen. Gulliver is obtuse in a plausible and often attractive way. He is a matter-of-fact man, capable of minute accuracy of detail in what he reports but equally capable of total indifference to the "value tone" of experience. His deadpan style is consistent understatement through much of the book. It is not knowing understatement such as we find in Hemingway, conscious of all it refuses to mention. It is, rather, unconscious irony—a style that is calculated (by Swift and not by Gulliver) to reveal sharply just those values it fails to observe or mention; a style that gives itself away. Swift's spokesmen are always chosen for this useful service: they cheerfully systematize, they avow what is commonly suppressed, they scandalize where wiser or more cautious men would draw back and reconsider.

Gulliver is invented as the hero of a comedy of incomprehension. This is only one dimension of *Gulliver's Travels,* but it is an essential one. Why comedy rather than satire? Because, in this one dimension, Gulliver embodies the incorrigible tendency of the mind to oversimplify experience, a trait that takes, with equal ease, the form of complacency or of misanthropy. Given his tendency to see man as either a rational animal or an irrational beast, given his expectation that man will be essentially good or essentially evil, Gulliver can never comprehend the problematic nature of man as he really is. As Swift sees him, man is both blessed and cursed with the condition of *animal rationis capax*. Because he is capable of reason man can at least glimpse

"Swift: Order and Obligation" by Martin Price. From To the Palace of Wisdom *(New York: Doubleday & Company, Inc., 1964), pp. 196–203. Copyright © 1964 by Martin Price. Reprinted by permission of the publisher.*

moral truth, because he is less than perfect in it he can lose the vision or pervert its meaning. The book raises the question of how much that we call civilization is an imperfect disguise of our lowest appetites (rather than a true sublimation or transformation of them), and also how far this civilization is necessary to the man who lives a purely moral life, adhering rigorously to the precepts of nature and reason alone (revelation apart). This is the same problem raised at least in passing by the *Argument against Abolishing Christianity.*

Finally, the book considers fundamental questions about the nature of politics, like the ideal reconciliation of duty and interest among the Houyhnhnms and the less perfect, but more humanly feasible, reconciliation in Brobdingnag. To these political orders are opposed such societies as that of the Lilliputians, which is elaborately administered disorder, the tyrannies of Laputa and Maldonada, and the savage democracy of the Yahoos. *Gulliver's Travels* is a tribute to the mixed state in which order is reconciled with freedom and yet made stable. To achieve such an order, one must come to terms with the nature of power, and the most essential feature of power is its tendency to become absolute.

Let us consider the political order. In Lilliput, Gulliver becomes the absolute weapon of an Emperor whose only wish is to conquer the world (that his world consists of two small islands makes the desire depressingly petty in its object but hardly petty in its intensity). The "spirit of opposition" governs the world of Lilliput; there is "a violent faction at home, and the danger [largely imaginary, a self-induced terror which unites the state, as in Orwell's *1984*] of an invasion by a most potent enemy from abroad" (I, iv). The occasions for dispute (like those for conquest) are so trivial as to be meaningless; the power drive creates its own pretexts. Within the state, the factions are rivals for influence and favor. Ministers are chosen by their agility—skill in walking a tightrope or jumping over sticks— and their subservience. The language of the court is a constant exercise in obfuscation. When the King's clemency is declared, his subjects run for cover. When Gulliver hastily puts out the fire in the Empress' palace by the quickest means available, the court accusation is a wonderful farrago of insinuation, self-importance, and intolerable legal jargon:

> Whereas . . . it is enacted that whoever shall make water within the precincts of the royal palace shall be liable to the pains and penalties of high treason: notwithstanding, the said Quinbus Flestrin [i.e., Gulliver], in open breach of the said law, under color of extinguishing the fire kindled in the apartment of his Majesty's most dear imperial consort, did maliciously, traitorously, and devilishly, by discharge of his urine, put out the said fire kindled in the said apartment, lying and being within the

precincts of the said royal palace, against the statute in that case provided, etc., against the duty, etc. (I, vii).

Or again Gulliver is accused of preparing to make a voyage to Blefuscu, "for which he hath received only verbal licence from his Imperial Majesty."

What is even more telling than the crazy mock logic of Lilliputian politics is Gulliver's readiness to adapt to it. A bluff, well-meaning Englishman, twelve times their size and able to destroy them with ease, he becomes dazzled by the honors paid him and the high status he has won at court. Gulliver is restrained in part by oath, in part by a sense of gratitude, but in part, too, by a naïve readiness to assume that power confers right. This becomes clear when, at the court of Brobdingnag, he reveals his belated schooling in Machiavellian statecraft and offers the horrified King the gift of gunpowder. Gulliver's disappointment at the rejection of this proposal is strong:

> A strange effect of narrow principles and short views! That a prince . . . should from a nice, unnecessary scruple, whereof in Europe we can have no conception, let slip an opportunity put into his hands, that would have made him absolute master of the lives, the liberties, and the fortunes of his people (II, vii).

In contrast to Lilliput, the Brobdingnagians have laws of no more than twenty-two words, and "to write a comment upon any law is a capital crime." Instead of a professional army they have a citizen militia, where "every farmer is under the command of his own landlord, and every citizen under that of the principal men in his own city, chosen after the manner of Venice by ballot" (II, vii). The militia fixes power in the whole body of the people rather than permitting the army to become an uncontrollable bloc such as we know in Latin-American politics today, and controls the disease that has attacked Brobdingnag, as it has every other nation: "the nobility often contending for power, the people for liberty, and the King for absolute dominion."

In the land of the Houyhnhnms we find an anarchy of reasonable creatures, such as William Godwin admired. The rational horses need no government; they immediately intuit their duties and perform them. Only in a rare instance, where a novel situation is created—as by Gulliver's presence—must they deliberate. They control any dissidence by rational persuasion and "exhortation," for they need no compulsion. George Orwell is interesting but, I think, mistaken when he sees in this exhortation the "totalitarian tendency which is explicit in the anarchist or pacifist vision of Society. In a Society in which there is no law, and in theory no compulsion, the only arbiter of behavior is public opinion,"—which Orwell shrewdly remarks, "is less

tolerant than any system of law." [1] This might be true if the Houyhnhnms cultivated a "general will," or if they carried on the kind of
virtuous terrorism that in schools often goes by the name of "honor
system." But there is no need to exert "continuous pressure" for conformity among the Houyhnhnms. They cannot but agree in all but
an occasional matter, and even in the case Swift presents the Houyhnhnm master hesitates to assent only because of Gulliver's furious
resistance to being sent away. Other critics have made similar objections about the religion of the Houyhnhnms. But one cannot call
them conformists, as Orwell does, or Deists, as others do. Their reason
inevitably produces agreement, and their piety is exemplary within
the limits of their purely natural reason. We cannot blame them for
finding fulfillment in what, for us, would be defects of liberty or fail-
ures of Christian faith.

Why should Swift have created these problems for us? Clearly he
is demanding of his readers what he never grants to Gulliver, the
power to make necessary distinctions. We must separate the intuitive
rightness of the Houyhnhnms' choice from the tyranny of conformity,
and we must separate natural piety from rationalistic or anti-clerical
deism. Gulliver fails to make the most important distinction of all
—between *animal rationale* and *animal rationis capax*. Only after
long exposure to human folly and perversity does he give up the
dream of man as a rational animal, but instead of coming to terms
with what in fact he is, Gulliver immediately turns to truly rational
animals, the Houyhnhnms, and hopes to become one of them. His
pathetic whinny and canter betray the fantasy of a literal-minded
convert.

The same kind of problem occurs in the realm of politics. Gulliver's
account of English institutions to the King of Brobdingnag betrays
the corruptibility they invite: English laws are extremely complex,
and they "are best explained, interpreted, and applied by those whose
interest and abilities lie in perverting, confounding, and eluding them"
(II, vi). There is no reconciliation of duty and interest, but instead
a systematic perversion of duty by interest. In his account of Europe
to his Houyhnhnm master, Gulliver makes explicit all that he has
earlier unconsciously revealed. Lawyers are now "equally disposed to
pervert the general reason of mankind in every other subject of discourse, as in that of their own profession" (IV, v). This single instance
is typical of all the rest. Gulliver has come to recognize the nature of
corruption, but his recognition is so belated and so passionate that he
despairs of all politics. When he writes an account of his travels, he
expects the world to reform at once. But, in this case at least, we have

[1] "Politics in Literature: An Examination of *Gulliver's Travels*," in *Shooting an
Elephant and Other Essays*, 1950.

a third possibility firmly sketched in: the reformed mixed state of the Brobdingnagians, which mediates between duty and interest, conformity and freedom, and accepts the need for a power structure but diffuses its control.

Parallel to the political issues in the book is the relationship of body and reason. In Lilliput, Gulliver's body is grosser than he can imagine (although he senses it), and the Lilliputians seem more delicate than in fact they are. In Brobdingnag the human body becomes monstrous, as Gulliver confronts with microscopic acuteness its ugliness and its noisome smells. In both the Struldbruggs and the Yahoos we see bodies that are completely without control or cleanliness; in fact, the Yahoos revel in filth and use excrement as a weapon. The body becomes a physical symbol of the power drives that are seen in the body politic; in Brobdingnag there is ugliness (simply more visible to Gulliver because of his diminutive size, as his own normal human ugliness was apparent to the Lilliputians) as there is cruelty and at least some measure of corruption (the farmer's turning Gulliver into a profitable show, the court dwarf's malice), but there is also a saving control of both corruption and physical nastiness. In the Struldbruggs old age has produced physical deterioration, avarice, contentiousness, and irrationality; in the Yahoos (who seem to have degenerated from an original couple, like the human race) there is sheer abandoned animality. The Yahoos are particularly nasty animals, it should be noted, not because Swift "in his fury . . . is shouting at his fellow-creatures: 'You are filthier than you are!' " (Orwell's view) but because they are a degenerate species, which neither possesses the instinctive controls of other animals (such as seasonal mating) nor preserves the faculties by which the human animal controls itself— its rational powers. Recent experiments have shown us animals that lose the power to identify with their proper kind and cannot acquire the traits of the kind they are raised among. Something of the sort has happened to the Yahoos; and their nastiness is only a further tribute to the importance of man's rational powers of self-control.

A third pattern, related to both politics and the control of the physical body, is that of simplicity and complexity. The Brobdingnagian laws are transparently simple; the Houyhnhnms need no laws at all. So it is with their cultures. The King, whose largeness of vision has the generosity of a Renaissance humanist, reminds us that Brobdingnag is a place of cultivation. But his people do not create books in great quantity; their largest library has a thousand volumes. In their writing "they avoid nothing more than multiplying unnecessary words, or using various expressions." They are skilled in practical arts, but utterly resistant to "ideas, entities, transcendentals, and abstractions." We see the reverse of this throughout the third voyage—

the elaborate astronomy of Laputa is coupled with infantile super-stition, the futile ingenuity of the experiments of Lagado is set against the simple adherence to traditional forms of Lord Munodi, the wisdom of Homer or Aristotle is swallowed up by the host of commentators that has battened on each. In place of the typical conqueror-heroes of history, Gulliver learns to admire the destroyers of tyrants and the defenders of liberty, the men who retrench corruption and win perse-cution in the process.

In the fourth voyage, the complexity of European civilization is traced in the Yahoos' savage behavior: they have a Prime Minister, they have court flirtations, they are acquisitive hoarders of shining stones, they become drunk and diseased, they even have a fashionable psychosomatic malady like the spleen. All the evils of civilization, and many of its professed glories, are caught in their elaborate behavior. In contrast, the Houyhnhnms perform "the necessary actions" of "a reasonable being" (IV, viii). They believe that "*reason* alone is suffi-cient to govern a *rational* creature"; they cannot even comprehend the nature of lies, let alone worse vices. "Neither is *reason* among them a point problematical as with us, where man can argue with plausibility on both sides of a question; but strikes you with immediate convic-tion, as it must needs do where it is not mingled, obscured, or dis-colored by passion and interest" (IV, viii). The consequences of per-fect rational intuition are acute. They have no parental partiality nor do they mate except to bear children, and their choice of a marriage partner is based on cool eugenic principles. They accept death as natural ripeness and a return to the first mother. What are we to make of this passionless simplicity, where all is governed by the impartial virtues of friendship and benevolence?

In recent years critics have tended increasingly to find in the Hou-yhnhnms a satire upon the neo-Stoic humanism of Shaftesbury or the Deists. It is true that Swift mocks those who would base their lives on the belief that virtue is its own reward, but he does not mock the moral intuition that the Houyhnhnms live by. Of course, the Hou-yhnhnms are not human, and Swift never could have intended that we treat them as models. They are like that return to the System of the Gospels with which the *Argument against Abolishing Christianity* teases us. It would be disastrous to "our present schemes of wealth and power." But could we, in fact, return to primitive Christianity? In *A Tale of a Tub,* when the two brothers reject the corruptions intro-duced by the third, Jack performs a thorough reformation on his coat and tears it to shreds. Martin, on the other hand, preserves those additions that cannot be removed without destroying the fabric. So here, Swift mocks us with all we are not, with the simplicity and direct acceptance of obligation that is given all the more weight in the teaching of the Gospels (unknown to the merely "natural" Houyhnhnms), and with the close resemblance of our vaunted civilization to the bestiality of the Yahoos. But it is Gulliver, in his despair, who draws from this recognition the resolution to become a Houyhnhnm, and it is this that makes him shrink as if from a Yahoo when he encounters the generous and humane Portuguese sea captain who brings him back to Europe. At the last, even with his family, he is alienated, morose, contemptuous, although he has slowly begun to adapt himself once more to the human condition.

Swift is neither offering the Houyhnhnms as a model nor holding them up for satire. They have, it is true, some telltale complacency in the conclusions they draw without sufficient fact. But when Swift defends the ancient poets against ridicule, he points out that their moral teachings were altogether admirable within the limits of their awareness.

The Houyhnhnms would make a ludicrous model for man, but it is Gulliver who makes them that. They remain an embodiment—in alien animal form—of the life of unclouded moral intuition; a simple life because there are no passions to produce conflict or to generate "opinion." In most telling contrast to them is the Academy of Lagado, with its technical extravagance, its furious dedication to doing the unnecessary with the most dazzling ingenuity, its constant rediscovery of brute fact through ludicrous failure. The scientist who places the bellows to the posterior of a dog and inflates the beast until it explodes in a torrent of excrement serves as a link between the learning of Lagado and the filth of the Yahoos.

The Houyhnhnms represent the order of mind at its purest, free of rationalistic system-building or of pride in intellectual constructions. Conceived in this way, it contains much that is given to humans only in the order of charity—a moral sureness and serenity, a spontaneous goodness such as is bred in men by a "daily vision of God." But to achieve the equivalent in the world of men requires the arduous self-scrutiny, the courageous defiance of the world, the saving humility that Pope seeks to dramatize in the *Imitations of Horace*.

PART TWO

View Points

W. L. Phelps: A Note on Gulliver

[Swift] may have taken horses as the ideal because England—much more than any other country—is the land of horses, where this animal is understood and appreciated. There is an enormous difference between England and America in the respective attention paid to these quadrupeds. There is not a single horse-race in America that is in any sense a national event, like the Derby in England. Nor does any-one—outside of those few specially interested—ever hear horse-racing discussed, as one hears baseball, tennis, football, and prize-fighting. I have never heard anyone in any American club mention horse-racing. George Moore's "Esther Waters" was a revelation to Americans of the English obsession.

Perhaps it is not too fanciful for me to suggest that another reason for taking the Houyhnhnms is because their language and inflection are so similar to the speech of English gentlemen. H. G. Wells in "Christina Alberta's Father" mentions an Englishman with one of these "whinnying voices," an absolutely accurate description, the voice beginning high and hesitating, and descending in cascades of sound.

From The Yale Review, *17 (1927), 96–97.*

Marjorie Nicolson and N. M. Mohler: The Scientific Background of Swift's *Voyage to Laputa*

The same trick of combining two sources[1] is found in the remarkable experiment of the projector who was able to make silk stockings and gloves from spiders' webs. Swift's projector was found in a room "where the walls and ceiling were all hung round with cobwebs." [2] He lamented "the fatal mistake the world had been so long in of

From Annals of Science, *2 (1937), 325–27. Copyright © 1937 by Taylor & Francis, Ltd. Reprinted by permission of Taylor & Francis, Ltd.*

[1] [I.e. combining two experiments like those reported in the *Philosophical Transactions* of the Royal Society.]

[2] *Voyage to Laputa*, p. 214 [ed. W. A. Eddy, 1933. Bk. III, ch. 5].

using silk-worms, while we had such plenty of domestic insects, who
infinitely excelled the former, because they knew how to weave as
well as spin." One critic has suggested that this idea went back to the
proposal of a Frenchman;[3] but it has not been noticed that that
Frenchman's proposal appeared in the *Philosophical Transactions*,
whence it came to Swift's attention. In a paper on "The Silk of Spiders,"
M. Bon in 1710 first gave an account of various sorts of spiders, which
reminds the English reader of the satirical interest in these insects in
Shadwell's earlier parody.[4] Shadwell's Sir Nicholas Gimcrack had become intimately acquainted with many kinds of spiders; but M. Bon
was concerned only with two: "*viz.* such as have long legs, and such
as have short Ones: The latter of which furnishes the Silk I am going
to speak of." M. Bon, however, was aware, as was Sir Nicholas Gimcrack, that spiders "are distinguished by their Colour, some being
Black, others Brown, Yellow, Green, White, and others of all these
Colours mixed together." Unlike Sir Nicholas Gimcrack, M. Bon was
less concerned with species of spiders than with their utilitarian value.
He wrote:

> The first Thread that they wind is weak, and serves them for no other
> Use than to make that Sort of Web, in which they catch Flies: The second
> is much stronger than the first; in this they wrap up their Eggs, and by
> this means preserve them from the Cold, and secure them from such
> Insects as would destroy them. These last Threads are wrapt very loosely
> about their Eggs, and resemble in Form the Bags of Silk-Worms, that have
> been prepared and loosened between the Fingers, in order to be put upon
> the Distaff. These Spiders Bags (if I may so call them) are of a grey
> Colour when they are new, but turn blackish when they have been long
> exposed to the Air. It is true, one may find several other Spiders Bags of
> different Colours, and that afford a better Silk, especially those of the
> Tarantula; but the Scarcity of them would render it very difficult to make
> Experiments upon them; so that we must confine ourselves to the Bags of
> such Spiders as are most common, which are the short-legg'd Ones. . . .
> And by getting together a great many of these Bags, it was that I made
> this new Silk, which is no-way inferior in Beauty to common Silk. It
> easily takes all sorts of Colours; and one may as well make large Pieces of
> it, as the Stockings and Gloves which I have made . . . .[5]

Only one significant difference appears in Swift's account. M. Bon
still found it necessary to dye his stockings and gloves in the usual way.
But the projector of Lagado had had access to another paper in the

---

[3] Émile Pons, *Gulliver's Travels* [1927], p. 254 n.
[4] [Thomas Shadwell's play, *The Virtuoso*, 1676. Sir Nicholas Gimcrack is the
name of the title character.]
[5] *Philosophical Transactions*, 1710, 27, 10.

Philosophical Transactions and was able to produce colours without added expense by a natural method:

> He proposed farther that by employing spiders the charge of dyeing silks should be wholly saved, whereof I was fully convinced when he showed me a vast number of flies most beautifully coloured, wherewith he fed his spiders, assuring us that the webs would take a tincture from them; and as he had them of all hues, he hoped to fit everybody's fancy, as soon as he could find proper food for the flies, of certain gums, oils, and other glutinous matter to give a strength and consistence to the threads.[6]

This trick Swift learned from another paper in the *Transactions,* of the very sort that must have delighted his ironic mind. Here Dr. Wall, beginning with a discourse on amber and diamonds, concluded with gum-lac, pismires and artificial and natural dyes, and unconsciously gave rise to experimentation in Lagado:

> I don't know in the Animal Kingdom any Thing but Pismires, that affords a Volatile Acid, and in the East-Indies there's a large kind of them that live on the Sap of certain Plants, affording both a Gum and a Colour, which Sap passing through the Body of those Insects and Animals, is by their Acid Spirit converted into an Animal Nature; which is the Reason, that with the Colour extracted from Gum-Lac (which Gum-Lac is nothing else but the Excrements of these Insects or Animals) almost as good, and full as lasting, Colours are made as from Cochineal: I am the more confirmed herein, because I know of an Artificial Way of converting Vegetable Colours into an Animal Nature very much like this, by which the Colours are made much more pleasant and permanent. After the same Manner the remaining Gum, which is an Oleosum, being digested and passing through the Bodies of those Insects or Animals, is by their Volatile Acid converted into a Vegetable Animal Phosphorus or Noctiluca.[7]

[6] *Voyage to Laputa,* p. 214 [Bk. III, ch. 5].
[7] *Phil. Trans.,* 1708, 26, 69.

G. *Wilson Knight:* Swift and the Symbolism of Irony

Gulliver's Travels, however plain and realistic its surface, depends likewise on a symbolic, sensory-physical structure. Books I and II use people either dwarf-like or vast. And the logic within this imaginative structure repays exact attention. Compare with Shakespeare's and Milton's feeling for kingship this description of the King of Lilliput:

From *Poets in Action* by *G. Wilson Knight (London: Methuen & Co., Ltd., 1967).* Reprinted by permission of the publisher.

He is taller by almost the breadth of my nail than any of his court, which alone is enough to strike an awe into the beholders. His features are strong and masculine, with an Austrian lip and arched nose, his complexion olive, his countenance erect, his body and limbs well-proportioned, all his motions graceful, and his deportment majestic. (Ch. II.)

And his proclamation:

Golbasto Momaren Evlame Gurdilo Shefin Mully Ully Gue, most mighty Emperor of Lilliput, delight and terror of the universe, whose dominions extend five thousand *blustrugs* (about twelve miles in circumference) to the extremities of the globe; monarch of all monarchs, taller than the sons of men; whose feet press down to the centre, and whose head strikes against the sun; at whose nod the princes of the earth shake their knees; pleasant as the spring, comfortable as the summer, fruitful as autumn, dreadful as winter . . . (Ch. III.)

These rely for their satiric force on our knowledge of his size. His *pride* is felt to be absurd—compare Pope's hatred of pride—when we remember his pigmy physique. Yet size is only relative. The King of England viewed by a hypothetical creature much larger would appear correspondingly small; but so, for that matter, would the larger person in similar plight—as indeed Gulliver himself does in Book II, where it is clearly stated that the King of England must have suffered similar indignities had he been there. So a sequence of bigger and bigger people can be imagined indefinitely. Swift has therefore, in playing with size, said precisely nothing. But see what has happened. Pride has been condemned, not by the author but by the reader. A new perspective reveals a truth which, once recognized, stands independent of any particular perspective: while, the recognition being our own, knowledge of the trick played on us will not invalidate it. Or we see that pride, so easily dethroned by an unreality, can only be so satirized since it depends on one. It is felt to be fundamentally a make-believe: whereas self-sacrifice, courage, simple good sense, are not: for all qualities in the book inherently praiseworthy do not appear invalidated at all. Something similar happens in Byron's otherwise very different *Don Juan*. The judgements are all the time our own—a thought I shall return to in discussion of Swift's irony—Swift merely forcing them to daylight recognition. This recognition is not always bitter, and may touch pure humour, comparable with that of Pope in *The Rape of the Lock*: as when, in Book II, after Gulliver's elaborate and proud exhibition of nautical skill in a tank with Glumdalclitch's breath for wind, the girl, it is quietly and unobtrusively observed, hangs the boat on a nail to dry. The humour depends on recognition of a possible context in which any pride may appear funny. Such ludicrous events condition, with Swift, true narrative power and sincerity, his admirable scheme leaving him nothing to do but the barest

description of—and this is characteristic—a simple *action*. Having
the right nouns ready, he has only to attach the verb. The power of
surface simplicity is fed entirely from the symbolism beneath.

Reliance on direct sensory-physical effects is greater in Book II than
Book I. Especially interesting is Swift's use of small animals of a
supposedly disgusting or absurd sort. The first Brobdingnagian he
meets looks on Gulliver as "a small dangerous animal" that may
"scratch" or "bite," such as a "weasel"; while Gulliver himself fears
he may be dashed to the ground as "any little hateful animal" a man
has a mind to destroy. The man's wife screams on seeing him as "at
the sight of a toad or a spider." When the boy is to be punished for
holding him up in air by the legs, Gulliver intercedes, remembering
a boy's natural mischievousness towards sparrows, rabbits, kittens,
and puppy dogs. To him a cat is now three times the size of an ox.
Gulliver's fight with the two rats is satirically heroic and his pride
ludicrous: especially when the maid picks up the dead one with a
pair of tongs and throws it out of the window. He sleeps in a doll's
cradle in a drawer. They consider him a *splacknuck*. Glumdalclitch
was once given a lamb which later went to the butcher and she fears
the same may happen to Grildrig. He is carried in a "box" with gimlet
holes to let in air. The dwarf, in professional jealousy, drops him into
a large bowl of cream, but, being a powerful swimmer, he survives.
His legs are also wedged by this dwarf during dinner into a marrow-
bone "where I stuck for some time, and made a very ridiculous figure."
Flies, "odious insects," trouble him, and he is admired for cutting
them in pieces with his knife. Fierce wasps steal his cake but he shows
courage in attack and "dispatches" four of them. There is the spaniel
carrying him in its mouth to its master, tail wagging. This was hushed
up: "And truly as to myself, I thought it would not be for my reputation that such a story should go about." A kite swoops down on him,
he falls into a mole-hill, breaks his shin by tumbling over a snail-shell.
He fights a thrush that snatched a piece of cake from his hand, but
the birds beat him off and return to hunt for "worms" and "snails."
He throws a "thick cudgel" at a linnet, and, knocking it down, runs
"with triumph" to his "nurse," but the bird recovers and causes great
trouble. A frog gets into his boat and daubs his face and clothes
with its "odious slime." And then there is the monkey catching and
squeezing him and taking him on to the roof, feeding him with food
from its own mouth, patting him when he will not eat. And all this
is built into that explicit statement of the king who sees Gulliver's
kind as "the most pernicious race of little odious vermin that nature
ever suffered to crawl upon the face of the earth."

I apologize for this rather obvious list. But observe its emphasis on
actions. Swift follows the Shakespearian tradition of nauseating ani-

mals: spiders, toads, monkeys, etc. The experience is similar to that
Shakespeare projects into *Othello*. The comparisons aim at outlining
sense of both indignity and disgust. The substance is to this extent
quite non-rational, and of an immediate and sensory sort, however it
may be used to blend with rational thinking.

J. R. Moore: The Geography of *Gulliver's Travels*

It is a commonplace that *Gulliver's Travels* is patterned after the
real voyages of Swift's age, which it either travesties or imitates. It
lacks the supplement, describing the flora and fauna, so often ap-
pended to voyages; but it has the connecting links of detailed narrative,
the solemn spirit of inquiry into strange lands, the factual records of
latitude and coasts and prevailing winds, and (most of all) *the
maps.* . . .

According to a letter to Swift, written November 8, 1726, Dr.
Arbuthnot "lent the book to an old gentleman, who went immediately
to his map to search for Lilliput." [1] That old gentleman is now
presumably dead; the results of his investigation are long overdue. . . .
In the latest critical edition of *Gulliver's Travels* the editor informs
us that

> Swift took a great deal of pains to make these sections of the narrative
> as plausible and circumstantial as possible. . . . Swift was bold enough
> to supply fairly exact data concerning the positions of these countries,
> although two errors (in the first chapter of the first voyage and the
> first chapter of the third voyage) and an insufficiently detailed para-
> graph in the next to the last chapter of the fourth voyage have led
> to some misunderstanding. . . . If this initial error is corrected all the
> rest of the geographical data which have caused confusion fall neatly
> into place. . . . the geography, was carefully worked out, . . . [2]

These assumptions of the essential accuracy of the geography of
Gulliver's Travels are groundless. Not only are the fanciful regions of
Brobdingnag and Laputa quite unlike those shown on the maps of
the First Edition; even if we allow for all possible errors from slips
of unsupervised printers in faraway London, and for the probability
of still greater errors from editorial attempts to correct the text, the
geography of the book is so incredible that we must assume (1) that
Swift intended an extravagant burlesque on voyages, or (2) that he

From Journal of English and Germanic Philology, *40 (1941), 214–20. Copyright ©
1941 by the University of Illinois Press. Reprinted by permission of the publisher.*

[1] Swift's *Correspondence* (ed. F. E. Ball), III, 358.

[2] *Gulliver's Travels*, ed. A. H. Case (New York, 1938), pp. 350–52. I have quoted
only excerpts, but I have not distorted the sense.

was ignorant of geography, or (3) that he intended a burlesque and knew too little geography to carry it out accurately. . . .

Gulliver reported that the dominions of Brobdingnag reached "about six thousand miles in length, and from three to five in breadth." [3] Mr. G. R. Dennis annotated this with a very cautious remark that "It will be noticed that on the map Brobdingnag is made very much smaller; but, as Sir Henry Craik suggests, this may be due to the engravers." [4]

Precisely so. On leaving Brobdingnag Gulliver was picked up by a vessel which had reached a longitude of 143° E. and a latitude of 44° N.,[5] and he was told that he was at least a hundred leagues from any land.[6] The eagle which had carried him southward from the southern extremity of Brobdingnag had presumably brought him from a latitude of approximately 50°. At that latitude the lessening of the earth toward the North Pole has become so considerable that *a degree of longitude* (which amounts to 69 statute miles at the equator) *has lessened to approximately 45 miles.* Six thousand miles, at 45 miles to the degree, would extend for about 133° of longitude, or considerably more than a third of the way around the globe on the fiftieth parallel. The ship's captain had reached a longitude of 143° E. before rescuing Gulliver. If the eastern end of Brobdingnag lay directly north of there, the western extremity would lie due north of Hamburg. If the western end of Brobdingnag lay in a longitude of 143° E., the eastern limit would be somewhere north of Saginaw, Michigan. . . .

As the other voyages do not lead to Brobdingnag, they cannot be expected to furnish such Gargantuan dimensions; but all were, in their way, incredible enough. The piratical crew of the fourth voyage, who sailed on past the Cape of Good Hope for the explicit purpose of marooning their captain, were not satisfied with putting Gulliver off at one of the usual landing places for pirates on or near Madagascar. They went on and on, out of any known course, until they confessed that they had no idea where they were,[7] and put him off some 4,000 nautical miles or more (or, if we accept the suggestion that he was marooned near the southeast end of Tasmania, some 6,000 miles) east of the Cape, by far the longest voyage of the sort in the annals of piracy. If the land of the Houyhnhnms was where Gulliver *seemed* to place it, west of the southwestern extremity of Australia, he was able, in leaving the country, to travel 1,500 or 2,000 nautical miles eastward

---

[3] *Gulliver's Travels*, ed. G. R. Dennis (London, 1899), p. 113. All citations are to this edition unless otherwise indicated—[Bk. II, ch. 4].

[4] *Loc. cit.*

[5] *Ibid.*, p. 153 [Bk. II, ch. 8].

[6] *Ibid.*, p. 150 [Bk. II, ch. 8].

[7] *Gulliver's Travels*, pp. 231, 295—[Bk. IV, chs. 1, 11].

in a canoe of stitched Yahoo skins, *in an actual sailing time of sixteen hours at a speed which he estimated at no more than a league and a half an hour.*[8] To be sure, Gulliver had a "very favourable wind," but his "little sail" was obviously some sort of magic carpet.

[8] *Ibid.,* p. 294 [Bk. IV, ch. 11].

Roland Mushat Frye: Swift's Yahoos and the Christian Symbols for Sin

Christian symbolism has traditionally used "the flesh" as representative of man's natural propensity towards evil. Bishop Gilbert Burnet, in his *Exposition of the Thirty-Nine Articles* (1699), writes in support of Article IX, "Of Original or Birth Sin," that "it is certain that in Scripture this general corruption of our nature is often mentioned." He then proceeds to quote nine typical passages which emphasize man's natural proclivity for evil, and concludes in this wise:

> The flesh is weak. The flesh lusteth against the spirit. The carnal mind is enmity to the law of God, and is not subject to the law of God, neither indeed can be: and they that are in the flesh cannot please God: *where by* flesh *is meant the natural state of mankind, according to those words,* That which is born of the flesh is flesh, and that which is born of the Spirit is spirit.[1]

Such was the conventional division of man for admonitory purposes, with the spirit as the valuable, redeeming part, and the flesh representing all the natural inclinations to evil which warred against the higher powers.

The most definite and most complete identification of the Yahoo with Gulliver is in terms of the flesh or the body. This is clearly stated when Gulliver is first able to inspect "the beast" at close range. "My Horror and Astonishment are not to be described," he says, "when I observed, in this abominable Animal, a perfect human Figure."[2] Later, Gulliver's master among the Houyhnhnms similarly observes that Gulliver "agreed in every Feature of [his] Body with other *Yahoos*" (pp. 243–44).[3] This perfect correspondence between

From Journal of the History of Ideas, *XV, 2 (1954), 205–16. Copyright © 1954 by* Journal of the History of Ideas. *Reprinted by permission of the author and the editor.*

[1] Gilbert Burnet, *An Exposition of the Thirty-Nine Articles* (London, 1850), p. 132.
[2] *Gulliver's Travels,* ed. Herbert Davis and Harold Williams (Oxford, 1941), 213–14 [Bk. IV, ch. 2].
[3] [Bk. IV, ch. 7.]

man and Yahoo in the body is even further emphasized by an elaboration of how they differ. Man differs in having the gift of speech and in having some faculty of reason, even though he does abuse it. There are other minor differences, but throughout the book the reiterated identification is physical. After the episode at the river when he is the object of fleshly desire, Gulliver says "I could no longer deny, that I was a real *Yahoo, in* every Limb and Feature, since the Females had a natural Propensity to me as one of their own Species." [4] The consistent reference is to physical similarities—in short, only one correlation seems valid, that Yahoo is man in "the flesh." . . .

The Yahoo may not only be related to Christian symbolism of the flesh, but may also be seen as embodying many of those elements of filth and deformity which are emblematic of sin throughout the Scriptures, beginning with the Levitical pollutions and carrying on far into the New Testament. Nor did Swift introduce the *literary* employment of dung, deformity and corruption, as is evident if we recall terms used in Milton's descriptions of Sin in *Paradise Lost,* and in Spenser's stripping of Duessa in *The Faerie Queene.*[5] To illustrate the vitality of this tradition in England, let me begin with three examples from the pulpit. I submit that if Swift had been guilty of any one of these statements, it would have been cited innumerable times as proof of his diseased outlook. In one of his Lincoln's Inn sermons, John Donne describes man's condition in this way: "Between that excremental jelly that thy body is made of at first, and that jelly which thy body dissolves to at last; there is not so noisome, so putrid a thing in nature." [6] Such, according to Donne, is man's mortal condition. Writing in 1667, B. Agas describes the godless who professed to be Christians: "As dross among Gold, or as scum upon a pot, such are these, a meer filth among the pure professors. They are the Gospels reproach and Religions shame, equally disgracing both the one and the other, as a dead blasted limb a living Body, or as a loathsome leperous scab a beautiful face." [7] In the same vein, Jeremie Taylor (1613–67) asks in his *Contemplation of the State of Man*: "What is man but a vessel of dung, a stink of corruption, and, by birth, a slave of the devil?" [8] Filth is employed in each of these three passages, in two of which terms for excrement are used. Two also employ a noisome or stinking smell as characteristic of evil, while a third adds the deformity of body and of face. . . .

---

[4] *Gulliver's Travels,* p. 251 [Bk. IV, ch. 8].

[5] *Paradise Lost,* II, 650–66, 795–800; X, 629–37, and *The Faerie Queene,* I, viii, 46–48.

[6] John Donne, *Works* (London, 1839), IV, 231.

[7] B. Agas, *Gospel Conversation, with a short Directory Thereunto* (London, 1667), 47.

[8] Taylor, *The Whole Works* (London, 1880), I, 396.

The very words used by Swift in describing the Yahoo are throughout strikingly like—and frequently identical with—those used by the theologians in treating "the flesh" and the sins to which it incites man. Compare with Swift's terms, as summarized above, these words already quoted from the theologians: deformity, brute, beast, animal, monster, excremental, dung, filth, stink, noisome, putrid, vile, loathsome, detestable. Such a close convergence cannot be explained away as fortuitous.

The correspondence, however, can be drawn even closer. The Yahoos may be seen, in almost every aspect of their being, in terms of the laws of pollution in the Old Testament. The food of the Yahoos, with certain exceptions (roots, berries, fish), is definitely polluting. Let us analyze their diet. They eat asses' flesh, battle for the possession of a dead cow, feed upon "the corrupted Flesh of Animals" and other carrion, kill and devour cats and dogs, as well as "Weasels and *Luhimuhs* (a Sort of *wild* Rat)." [9] Each one of these delicacies is proscribed as polluting under the Levitical code. Leviticus 11.3 prohibits the eating of asses' flesh, and in the thirty-ninth and fortieth verses of the same chapter the consumption of any meat from a dead carcass, whether that of a clean or unclean animal, is forbidden. The twenty-seventh verse declares that cats and dogs are unclean. Finally, weasels and rodents are prohibited in the twenty-ninth verse.[10] Thus we see that in diet the Yahoos are guilty of those defilements "whereby either the *Guilt* or the *Disorder* of Sin . . . are represented."

[9] *Gulliver's Travels*, 213, 214, 244, 245, 250, and 255 [Bk. IV, chs. 2, 7, 8, 9].
[10] Simon Patrick, *Commentary upon Leviticus* (London, 1698), 160, 186, and 179, confirms the currency of these interpretations in the age of Swift.

Paul Fussell: The Frailty of Lemuel Gulliver

Gulliver's clothing and personal property are perpetually suffering damage, and, when they are not actually being damaged, Gulliver is worrying that, at any moment, they may be. Of course, mindful of Crusoe's pathetic situation, we are not surprised that a shipwrecked mariner suffers damage to his clothing and personal effects. But we may be surprised to hear Gulliver go out of his way to call careful attention to the damages and losses he suffers. In the first voyage, for example, Gulliver circumstantially lets us know that his scimitar has rusted, that his hat has been sorely damaged by being hauled through the

From Essays in Literary History, ed. Rudolf Kirk and C. F. Main (New Brunswick: Rutgers University Press, 1960), pp. 119–20. Copyright © 1960 by Rutgers, The State University. Reprinted by permission of the publisher.

dust all the way from the sea to the capital, and that his breeches have suffered an embarrassing rent. The boat in which Gulliver escapes to Blefuscu is, we are carefully told, "but little damaged." Once off the islands and, we might suppose, secure from losses and accidents until his next voyage, Gulliver loses one of his tiny souvenir sheep—it is destroyed by a rat aboard ship.

Presumably outfitted anew, Gulliver arrives ashore in Brobdingnag with his effects intact, but the old familiar process of damage and deterioration now begins all over again. Wheat beards rip his clothes; a fall into a bowl of milk utterly spoils Gulliver's suit; his stockings and breeches are soiled when he is thrust into the marrow bone which the queen has been enjoying at dinner; his clothes are again damaged by his tumble into the mole hill; and his suit (what's left of it) is further ruined by being daubed by frog slime and "bemired" with cow dung. Likewise, in the third voyage, our attention is called to the fact that Gulliver's hat has again worn out, and in the fourth voyage we are informed yet again by Gulliver that his clothes are "in a declining Condition."

At times, in fact, Gulliver's clothes and personal effects seem to be Gulliver himself: this is the apparent state of things which fascinates the observing Houyhnhnm before whom Gulliver undresses, and this ironic suggestion of an equation between Gulliver and his clothing, reminding us of the ironic "clothes philosophy" of Section II of *A Tale of a Tub,* Swift exploits to emphasize that damage to Gulliver's naturalistic garments is really damage to the naturalistic Gulliver. The vulnerability of Gulliver's clothing, that is, is a symbol three degrees removed from what it signifies: damage to Gulliver's clothes is symbolic of damage to Gulliver's body, which, in turn, is emblematic of damage to Gulliver's self-esteem.

Jim W. Corder: Gulliver in England

The land of the Houyhnhnms is after all a familiar setting—England, seen by a distorting eye. In Chapter Eight, wherein Gulliver relates "several Particulars of the Yahoos," and describes the virtues, education, and exercise of the Houyhnhnm youth, he has occasion to speak of the quarterly tests which the youth of the land undergo:

> Four times a Year the Youth of certain Districts meet to shew the Proficiency in Running, and Leaping, and other Feats of Strength or Agility; where the Victor is rewarded with a Song made in his or

From College English, *23 (1961), 100–101. Copyright © 1961 by the National Council of Teachers of English. Reprinted by permission of the National Council of Teachers of English and Jim W. Corder.*

her Praise. On this Festival the Servants drive a Heard of *Yahoos* into the Field, laden with Hay, and Oats, and Milk for a Repast to the *Houyhnhnms;* after which, these Brutes are immediately driven back again, for fear of being noisome to the Assembly. (p. 220)[1]

Horse show, horse race, or what have you—this is England, with men tending to the horses before the exhibition. The Houyhnhnms are horses, not Utopians, and certainly one of the finest comic effects in the entire work is the eagerness with which the happy gull seizes on the life of the horse as ideal.

Other passages also reveal these fleeting images of England. Gulliver, speaking to his Master, mentions the horses that are kept in England, "where *Yahoo*-servants were employed to rub their Skins smooth, comb their Manes, pick their Feet, serve them with Food, and make their Beds." [2] The Houyhnhnm Master immediately understands that there is after all no difference between England and his own land—except, as the reader knows, for that point of view which reverses the position of master and servant and makes the English groom the horse's inferior. At another point, the Houyhnhnm mentions the repulsiveness of the Yahoo's diet: "Herbs, Roots, Berries, corrupted flesh of Animals"—the diet of humans, of course; or "all mingled together"—[3] a good English stew. Later in his discussions, the Master's description of the behavior of the female Yahoo is, if we remember whom we are hearing and under what conditions we hear him, an almost literal description of a belle in St. James Park. He describes, in fact, such a scene as we have often encountered in Restoration comedy:

> . . . a Female *Yahoo* would often stand behind a Bank or a Bush, to gaze on the young Males passing by, and then appear, and hide, using many antick Gestures and Grimaces; at which time it was observed, that she had a most *offensive Smell;* and when any of the Males advanced, would slowly retire, looking often back, and with a counterfeit Shew of Fear, run off into some convenient Place where she knew the Male would follow her. (p. 215)[4]

If one looks closely here, he can see the gestures of a lady with a fan, looking flirtatiously over her shoulder. He can also observe in the "offensive Smell" not just the sexual implication, but also, quite simply, the presence of perfume.

One last passage must be noted. Again in Chapter Eight Gulliver speaks of marriage among the Houyhnhnms:

---

[1] References are to Jonathan Swift, *Gulliver's Travels and Other Writings,* introduction by Ricardo Quintana (1958).

[2] [Bk. IV, ch. 4.]

[3] [Bk. IV, ch. 7.]

[4] [Bk. IV, ch. 7.]

In their Marriages they are exactly careful to chuse such Colours as will not make any disagreeable Mixture in the Breed. *Strength* is chiefly valued in the Male, and *Comeliness* in the Female; not upon the Account of *Love*, but to preserve the Race from degenerating: For, where a Female happens to excel in *Strength*, a Consort is chosen with regard to *Comeliness*. (p. 219)

Gulliver is impressed, as he is by most Houyhnhnm practices. Here the thing that impresses him is simply English horse breeding methods, seen the wrong way.

W. B. Carnochan: Some Roles of Lemuel Gulliver

Gulliver, at the beginning of his narrative, is the myopic hero whose lack of understanding is symbolized by the weakness and vulnerability of his eyesight. In Lilliput the only items which escape the inventory of his captors are his "Pocket Perspective" and the pair of spectacles "which I sometimes use for the Weakness of mine Eyes." And these are evidently the possessions by which he sets the most store. He keeps them in a secret pocket, and he explains with a trace of guilt that he did not surrender them to his captors because they were of "no Consequence" to the emperor; therefore, "I did not think my self bound in Honour to discover [them]; and I apprehended they might be lost or spoiled if I ventured them out of my Possession." (21)[1] Gulliver's caution turns out to be well advised: his spectacles later shield his eyes, which otherwise "I should have infallibly lost," (36)[2] from the arrows of Blefuscu. But the only way for Gulliver to shield his eyes—"and consequently my Liberty"—(57)[3] from the lenient workings of Lilliputian justice is by flight; and the official sentence of the council is the climax to the theme of sight and understanding in the first Book. Reldresal, who first proposes the idea of blinding the Man-Mountain as a humane alternative to capital punishment, defends his plan with these arguments (as reported to Gulliver by his informant from the court): "That the loss of your Eyes would be no Impediment to your bodily Strength, by which you might still be useful to his Majesty. That Blindness is an Addition to Courage, by concealing Dangers from us; that the Fear you had for your Eyes, was the greatest Difficulty in bringing over the Enemy's Fleet; and it would be sufficient for you to see by the Eyes of the Min-

From Texas Studies in Language and Literature, *5 (1964), 526–28. Copyright ©
1964 by University of Texas Press. Reprinted by permission of the publisher.*

[1] [All references are to the Davis-Williams edition, 1941. Bk. I, ch. 2.]
[2] [Bk. I, ch. 5.]
[3] [Bk. I, ch. 7.]

isters, since the greatest Princes do no more." (54)[4] At first Reldresal
speaks quite literally, although the metaphorical meaning of sight is always latent; in his last argument he lapses into pure metaphor, as
though unawares. And his sophistries remind us of the links between
weak sight and weak understanding. Since Gulliver is not a tragic
figure, however, he is spared the purgative blindness that sometimes
brings insight in the world of tragedy. In time, and with experience,
Gulliver comes to see more clearly; or, as some would argue, to think
he sees more clearly. In any case, it is himself he sees. The spectacles
and pocket perspective of Book I, which Gulliver uses to examine the
external world, give way in Brobdingnag and Houyhnhnmland to
reflecting surfaces in which Gulliver looks upon his own features—first
with chagrin, then with loathing, and finally with the hope of accepting what he sees.

Gulliver first glimpses himself early in his voyage to Brobdingnag,
and he joins the Brobdingnagians in their amusement at the sight:
"Neither indeed could I forbear smiling at my self, when the Queen
used to place me upon her Hand towards a Looking-Glass, by which
both our Persons appeared before me in full View together; and there
could be nothing more ridiculous than the Comparison." The result of
this first confrontation is to make Gulliver think that he is no longer
what he was before: "So that I really began to imagine my self dwindled
many Degrees below my usual Size." (91)[5] Like Alice, in Wonderland,
Gulliver has found that "being so many different sizes . . . is very con-
fusing"; and, like Alice, Gulliver would find it hard to answer the
Caterpillar's question: "Who are *you*?"[6] Self-abasement has begun,
and Gulliver tries now to avoid his reflection; it is painful, he discovers, to be laughable—a reminder, once more, of the Hobbesian theory
of laughter. When Gulliver is rescued from the sea, he tells the ship's
captain of his experiences in Brobdingnag and of his increasing self-
contempt, adding in an aside to the reader: "For, indeed, while I was
in that Prince's Country, I could never endure to look in a Glass after
mine Eyes had been accustomed to such prodigious Objects; because
the Comparison gave me so despicable a Conceit of my self." (131)[7]

Gulliver's feelings in Houyhnhnmland—his "Horror and detestation" when he catches sight of himself in a lake or fountain—are an
intensification, therefore, of feelings that he has first experienced in
Brobdingnag. Now Gulliver is taught by the Houyhnhnms to distrust
the powers of human reason; his master comes to the conclusion that
"instead of Reason, we were only possessed of some Quality fitted to

[4] [Bk. I, ch. 7.]
[5] [Bk. II, ch. 3.]
[6] *The Complete Works of Lewis Carroll* (New York, 1924), p. 54.
[7] [Bk. II, ch. 8.]

increase our natural Vices"; and he likens this quality to a troubled
stream that gives off distorted images of objects mirrored there—"as
the Reflection from a troubled Stream returns the Image of an ill-
shapen Body, not only *larger*, but more *distorted*"—(232)[8] a simile
that Swift may owe to a familiar passage in the *Novum Organum*:
"the human understanding is like a rough mirror, which mingles its
own nature with the rays of what it reflects, distorting and discoloring
the nature of things." Then the assault of the female Yahoo causes
Gulliver to see himself as a "real Yahoo, in every Limb and Feature"—
(251)[9] a conclusion that first seems unjustified. Might Gulliver not
have concluded equally well that he was a monkey in every limb and
feature after the parallel incident in Book II? But there is a difference.
Gulliver admits that he has stimulated the Yahoos to look on him as
one of their species by frequently "stripping up my Sleeves, and shew-
ing my naked Arms and Breast in their Sight." (249)[10] His exhibition-
ism in this case is overtly sexual (there seems no other interpretation);
and, despite his humiliation, Gulliver apparently feels some reciprocal
attraction to his Yahoo assailant: he remarks that she "did not make
an Appearance altogether so hideous as the rest of the Kind." (251)[11]
Thus bereft of pride of mind and pride of body, Gulliver understandably prefers the sight of a common Yahoo to the sight of himself. When
he returns home, however, his loneliness leads him eventually to look
for ways of coming to terms with mankind, and he decides that he
can no longer avoid the sight of what he is. He decides "to behold
my Figure often in a Glass, and thus if possible habituate my self by
Time to tolerate the Sight of a human Creature." (279)[12]

[8] [Bk. IV, ch. 5.]
[9] [Bk. IV, ch. 8.]
[10] [Bk. IV, ch. 8.]
[11] [Bk. IV, ch. 8.]
[12] [Bk. IV, ch. 12.]

Chronology of Important Dates

Swift's Life	General Events
	1660 Restoration of Charles II
1667 Born in Dublin, Nov. 30	
1686 B.A., Trinity College, Dublin	
	1687 Newton, *Principia Mathematica*
	1688 Glorious Revolution
	1690 Locke, *Essay Concerning Human Understanding*
1695 Ordained priest. Rector of Kilroot, Ireland	
	1700 Death of Dryden
1702 D.D., Trinity College, Dublin	1702 Accession of Queen Anne
1710 Edits Tory journal, *The Examiner*	
1711 *Argument against Abolishing Christianity*	1711 Shaftesbury, *Characteristics of Men and Manners*
1713 Dean of St. Patrick's Cathedral, Dublin	1713 Treaty of Utrecht
	1714 Accession of George I
	1715 Jacobite Rebellion
	1720 South Sea Bubble
	1721 Walpole made First Lord of the Treasury
1724 *The Drapier's Letters*	
1726 *Gulliver's Travels*	
	1727 Accession of George II
1729 *A Modest Proposal*	1729 Pope, *Dunciad,* first version
1731 *Verses on the Death of Dr. Swift* written (published 1739)	
	1738 Johnson, *London*
1742 "Of unsound mind and memory"; put under guardianship	
	1744 Death of Pope
1745 Died in Dublin, Oct. 19	

Notes on the Editor and Contributors

FRANK BRADY, the editor of this volume, teaches English at the City University of New York and is the author of *Boswell's Political Career*.

W. B. CARNOCHAN, author of several articles about Swift, teaches English at Stanford.

JIM W. CORDER, who teaches at Texas Christian, edited *Shakespeare 1964*.

The late R. S. CRANE, Distinguished Service Professor at the University of Chicago, was for many years editor of *Philological Quarterly*. He wrote *The Languages of Criticism and the Structure of Poetry*.

ROBERT C. ELLIOTT, who has held Ford and Guggenheim fellowships, teaches at the University of California at San Diego.

ROLAND MUSHAT FRYE has written *God, Man, and Satan: Patterns of Christian Thought and Life in "Paradise Lost"* and *Shakespeare and Christian Doctrine*. He is Professor of English at the University of Pennsylvania.

PAUL FUSSELL, Professor of English and Director of Graduate Studies at Rutgers, The State University, is also Secretary of the English Institute. His most recent book is *The Rhetorical World of Augustan Humanism*.

G. WILSON KNIGHT, Professor of English Literature Emeritus at Leeds University, is well known for his studies of Shakespeare and Byron.

SAMUEL H. MONK, author of *The Sublime: A Study of Critical Theories in XVIII-Century England* and editor of *Five Miscellaneous Essays by Sir William Temple*, teaches at Minnesota.

J. R. MOORE, a leading Defoe authority, is Distinguished Service Professor Emeritus at Indiana University.

MARJORIE NICOLSON, Trent Professor of English Emerita at Columbia, has written several books on science and literature in the seventeenth and eighteenth centuries. Her most recent work is *Pepys' "Diary" and the New Science*. N. M. MOHLER is professor of Physics Emerita at Smith College. One of her fields of interest is the history of physics.

The late W. L. PHELPS, once Lampson Professor of English at Yale, was one of the most eminent teachers of his era and an authority on Browning.

MARTIN PRICE, author of *Swift's Rhetorical Art*, teaches English at Yale.

E. W. ROSENHEIM is Professor of English at the University of Chicago.

HENRY W. SAMS is Professor of English and Head of the Department at the Pennsylvania State University.

MILTON VOIGT is Dean of the College of Letters and Science at the University of Utah.

T. O. WEDEL, at one time Professor of English at Carleton College, is Canon and Warden Emeritus of Washington Cathedral.

KATHLEEN WILLIAMS is Professor of English at the University of California at Riverside. Her most recent book is *Essays in this Soveraine Light.*

Selected Bibliography

The necessary brevity of this selection makes it highly arbitrary. A full bibliography for 1945–1965 can be found in J. J. Stathis, *A Bibliography of Swift Studies* (Nashville: Vanderbilt University Press, 1967). Works in the list below marked "in Tuveson" are printed, in whole or in part, in *Swift: A Collection of Critical Essays*, ed. Ernest Tuveson (Englewood Cliffs, N.J.: Prentice-Hall, Inc., 1964).

Ehrenpreis, Irvin, "The Meaning of Gulliver's Last Voyage," *Review of English Literature*, 3 (1962), 18–38. In Tuveson. The view of Swift's leading biographer.

Horrell, Joseph, "What Gulliver Knew," *Sewanee Review*, 51 (1943), 476–504. In Tuveson. Not always convincing, but very suggestive.

Kelling, H. D., "*Gulliver's Travels*: A Comedy of Humours," *University of Toronto Quarterly*, 21 (1952), 362–75. Gulliver seen as a character in the "humor" tradition of Ben Jonson.

Mack, Maynard, ed., *The Augustans*, 2nd ed. (Englewood Cliffs, N.J.: Prentice-Hall, Inc., 1961), pp. 14–16. In Tuveson. Some brief, acute remarks.

Orwell, George, "Politics and Literature: An Examination of *Gulliver's Travels*," *Shooting an Elephant and Other Essays* (London: Secker and Warburg, 1950). Interesting, as one major satirist's view of another.

Price, Martin, *Swift's Rhetorical Art* (New Haven: Yale University Press, 1953). The most subtle, and perhaps the finest, critical study of Swift.

Ross, J. F., "The Final Comedy of Lemuel Gulliver," *Studies in the Comic*, University of California Publications in English, Vol. 8, No. 2 (1941), 175–96. In Tuveson. The first extended modern study of *Gulliver's Travels*. Important.

Traugott, John, "A Voyage to Nowhere with Thomas More and Jonathan Swift: *Utopia* and *The Voyage to the Houyhnhnms*," *Sewanee Review*, 69 (1961), 534–65. In Tuveson. A brilliant, original view of *Gulliver's Travels* as a complex utopian exercise.

Watt, Ian, "The Ironic Tradition in Augustan Prose from Swift to Johnson," *Restoration and Augustan Prose* (Los Angeles: William Andrews Clark Memorial Library, 1956), pp. 19–46. Some perceptive comments, especially on Gulliver as character and *persona*.

Wilson, J. R., "Swift's Alazon," *Studia neophilologica*, 30 (1958), 153–64. A study of Gulliver as impostor.